how2become

ROYAL NAVY
RECRUITING (RT) TEST

www.How2Become.com

As part of this product you have also received FREE access to online tests that will help you to pass the Royal Navy Recruiting Test.

To gain access, simply go to:

www.PsychometricTestsOnline.co.uk

Get more products for passing any test or interview at:

www.how2become.com

Orders: Please contact How2become Ltd, Suite 2, 50 Churchill Square Business Centre, Kings Hill, Kent ME19 4YU.

You can order through Amazon.co.uk under ISBN 978-1-910602-15-7, via the website www.How2Become.com or through Gardners.com.

ISBN: 978-1-910602-15-7

First published in 2015 by How2become Ltd.

Typeset for How2become Ltd by Anton Pshinka.

Disclaimer

Every effort has been made to ensure that the information contained within this guide is accurate at the time of publication. How2become Ltd is not responsible for anyone failing any part of any selection process as a result of the information contained within this guide. How2become Ltd and their authors cannot accept any responsibility for any errors or omissions within this guide, however caused. No responsibility for loss or damage occasioned by any person acting, or refraining from action, as a result of the material in this publication can be accepted by How2become Ltd.

The information within this guide does not represent the views of any third party service or organisation.

CONTENTS

INTRODUCTION

INTRODUCTION TO YOUR NEW GUIDE

Welcome to your new guide, the Royal Navy Recruiting test: Practice tests for the Royal Navy selection process for Ratings. This guide contains 100s of pages of sample test questions that are appropriate for anyone who is applying to join the Royal Navy.

The selection tests for the Armed Forces are designed to assess potential employees 'suitability' for specific job posts. In the majority of cases, the higher scores you achieve, the more job opportunities you will have at your disposal. The key to success is to try your hardest to get 100% in the test that you are undertaking. If you aim for 100% in your preparation, then you are far more likely to achieve the trade or career that you want. We have deliberately supplied you with lots of sample questions to assist you in your preparation. It is crucial that when you get a question wrong, you take the time to find out why you got it wrong; understanding the question is very important!

Finally, we recommend that you obtain additional test questions for preparing to join the Royal Navy via our website www.how2become.com. From this website, you will be able to find our highly recommended **Armed Forces Test** book, which contains a further 250 pages worth of sample test questions to assist you. You will find that the more practice you undertake in the build up to the real test, the better you will perform on the day.

Good luck and best wishes.

The how2become team

The How2become team

STRUCTURE OF THE BOOK

We have provided you with eight testing sections, each with a variety of questions and levels of difficulty for you to work through. Work through each chapter and then check your answers with the detailed answers and explanations provided.

This comprehensive Royal Navy Recruiting test practice guide follows the structure as formulated below:

- Introduction – introducing your new guide
- About Royal Navy Recruiting tests
- Royal Navy Recruiting test – **Reasoning**
  - o Example Reasoning questions
  - o Test Sections 1 and 2
  - o Detailed answers and explanations
- Royal Navy Recruiting test – **Verbal Ability**
  - o Example Verbal Ability questions
  - o Test Sections 1 and 2
  - o Detailed answers and explanations
- Royal Navy Recruiting test – **Numerical Reasoning**
  - o Example Numerical questions
  - o Test Sections 1 and 2
  - o Detailed answers and explanations
- Royal Navy Recruiting test – **Mechanical Comprehension**
  - o Example Mechanical Comprehension questions
  - o Test Sections 1 and 2
  - o Detailed answers and explanations
- A Few Final Words…

ABOUT
THE ROYAL NAVY
RECRUITING TEST

ABOUT THE ROYAL NAVY RECRUITING TEST

Psychometric tests have been in use in the Armed Forces for many years. They are used to assess a candidate's ability to perform tasks similar to those they would face in real life scenarios. Ultimately, these tests have been designed to measure a person's abilities, skills, knowledge and mind-set, in order to determine how suitable they are for the Royal Navy.

ROYAL NAVY RECRUITING TEST (RT)

The Royal Navy Recruiting (RT) test will also evaluate your academic ability, to check which role within the Navy is the best fit for you. It does not matter what qualifications you have, you will still be required to sit the RT, and your results will go towards determining your suitability for the Armed Forces. Your performance in the RT will demonstrate your ability to cope with the technical and academic requirements of the Royal Navy training.

There are four separate parts of the test which you will need to complete and pass in order to move on to the next stage of the application process. These tests will measure your levels of:

- General Reasoning
- Verbal Ability
- Numerical Reasoning
- Mechanical Comprehension

WHY AM I BEING TESTED?

The main purpose of the Royal Navy Recruiting test is to establish how effective you are at figuring out problems, assess your English and Mathematical ability, and determine whether or not you are able to understand the basic mechanical concepts.

Psychometric tests are a useful way to decipher a person's level of intellectual, critical and technical ability. These tests evaluate a candidate's performance based on what they can achieve in an array of areas, and how they can cope with the technical and demanding nature within the Naval Service.

ABOUT THE TEST

The Royal Navy Recruiting test covers the following four areas which are conducted under **strict time limits**:

- A Reasoning test (30 questions to be completed in 9 minutes).

- A Verbal Ability test (30 questions to be completed in 9 minutes).

- A Numeracy test (30 questions to be completed in 16 minutes).

- A Mechanical Comprehension test (30 questions to be completed in 10 minutes).

The tests are usually carried out at the Armed Forces Careers Office and will be conducted under strict timed conditions. Details of the time limit and number of questions per exercise will be provided in your recruitment guide. Your recruitment guide is key! Make sure you take the time to thoroughly read through the whole booklet so you are fully aware of the expectations of your assessment. The pass mark for the Royal Navy Recruiting test will very much depend on the technical ability level required for the post for which you are applying; although a pass mark of 50% is normally sufficient for the majority of branches.

TIME LIMITS

For the duration of the test, you will be observed by an invigilator. A qualified member of the Naval Careers Service will provide instructions on how to complete the test before you begin.

The test is set under timed conditions; conditions which the majority of candidates find extremely limiting. Each sub-test has its own time limit, so you must pay attention to the time you have to complete the set number of questions in each sub-test.

- A Reasoning test (30 questions to be completed in 9 minutes).
- A Verbal Ability test (30 questions to be completed in 9 minutes).
- A Numeracy test (30 questions to be completed in 16 minutes).
- A Mechanical Comprehension test (30 questions to be completed in 10 minutes).

HOW CAN I PREPARE?

The only way to prepare for your Royal Navy Recruiting test, or any other form of psychometric testing, is through practising.

Practice is the best form of preparation. Most psychometric tests require you to be familiar with the concepts and testing layout, in order to stand a chance of successfully passing. Practicing will maximise your chances of success.

In order to succeed, you need to have a clear understanding of the expectations of the test. You need to know how to complete the question, so that it doesn't startle you on the day of your real test. All psychometric testing requires a great deal of commitment and perseverance, so you need to be fully committed to the job role for which you are applying.

Practicing beforehand will give you some indication of how well you will perform these tests under severe time constraints. As mentioned earlier, the test is set under extreme time limits; thus practicing will not only enable you to determine how well you perform under these time limits, but also helps to improve your logical ability and timing skills.

Finally, we have also provided you with some additional free online psychometric tests which will help to further improve your competence in this particular testing area. To gain access, simply go to:

www.PsychometricTestsOnline.co.uk

Good luck and best wishes,

The how2become team

The How2become team

ROYAL NAVY RECRUITING TEST – **REASONING**

As part of your Royal Navy Recruiting test, you will be required to take a Reasoning test; one of four sub-sections of your assessment.

Reasoning skills are assessed to determine a candidate's ability to process information and recognise underlying patterns and configurations amongst a set of words, shapes or sequences.

The Reasoning test will be in the format of both Verbal Ability and Diagrammatic Reasoning. In other words, some questions will require you to look at the relationships between words, sentence structures and patterns, whilst other questions will need you to focus on shape formations, recognising abstract imagery and spot correlations. Therefore, it is important that you fully comprehend both question types, and understand what is required for this part of the Royal Navy assessment.

On the day of your Royal Navy assessment, **you will have 9 minutes in which to answer the 30 questions** relating to Reasoning. In your real test, please note that you will be given a separate sheet of paper in which you indicate your answers, however for the purpose of this book, we would like you to indicate your answers underneath the question by highlighting or writing your answer.

In order to gain some understanding of the types of questions you will face during this sub-test, and how you should go about answering them, check out the following pages of example questions. These examples provide clear and detailed descriptions of how to answer the question correctly, what to expect, what to look out for, and useful tips regarding General Reasoning.

Good luck.

EXAMPLES OF
REASONING TEST

Complete the Pair

Look at how the figure changes from box 1 to box 2. Apply the same changes in order to get the correct answer.

Example:

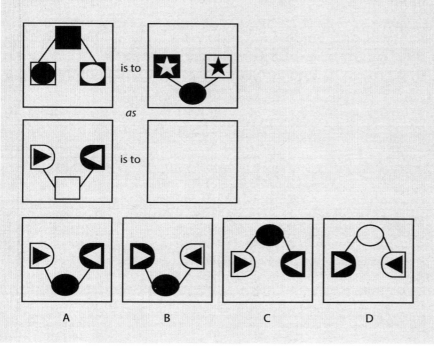

A   B   C   D

ANSWER = D

You have to decide which of the answer options fits with the overall sequence. There is a link between the first row of shapes and the second row of shapes. You need to make sure that you study the whole question carefully and use the same sequence pattern throughout.

Pay attention to everything! Colours, size, rotations, reflections, patterns, numbers. Anything could be changing in the sequence!

In the above question, in the top left box, you start with a black square. This links to a white square with a black circle, and a black square with a white circle. In the top right box, this changes, to the black square becoming a black circle (and its been moved to the bottom of the square). The white square with the black circle has become a black square with a white star. The black square with the white circle has become a white square with a black star.

The sequence alternates colour patterns. The colour in the first box changes to the opposite colour in the second box.

To work out the answer, the same rules apply for both sequences. The white square at the bottom of the page will become a black circle at the top. The shapes that are connected to this, remain the same, but the colour pattern changes. So whatever is white in the first box will become black and vice versa.

Complete the Sequence

Work out which option fits best in the missing square in order to complete the sequence.

Example:

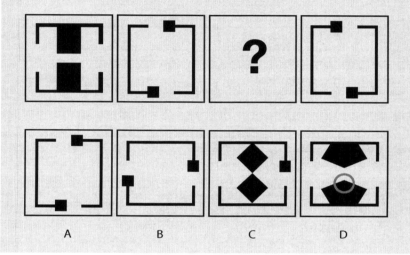

A   B   C   D

ANSWER = D

You need to pay close attention to how the sequence is progressing.

Pay attention to small details such as positioning, shapes, colours, numbers, rotations, symmetry.

In the above example, you will notice that in every even box (2 and 4), each shape is reflected horizontally. Box 1 and box 3 need to follow the same pattern. Box 1 contains a black shape inside open brackets, with no square on the outside. Therefore box 3 should also contain a black shape, inside open brackets, with no square on the outside.

Number Sequences

Work out which number completes the sequence.

Example:

7   10   14   19   25   ?

How to work it out:

- You need to find the pattern between each of the numbers. Sometimes there may only be one pattern (as shown in the above example), or sometimes there may be two patterns (as shown in the example below).

- In the example above, the numbers increase by 3, then 4, then 5, then 6, and so forth, so the next number in the sequence needs to be increased from 25 by 7, giving you the answer of 32.

Example:

3   5   5   10   7   15   ?

How to work out it out:

- In the second example, two patterns are occurring.

- Every odd number positioned in the sequence is increasing by 2 (3 + 2 = 5, 5 + 2 = 7 etc).

- Every even number positioned in the sequence is a multiple of 5.

- So the next number in the sequence is an odd number (its position in the sequence is number 7), therefore it will follow the pattern of being increased by 2 from the previous odd number.

- So, 7 + 2 = 9. So, the next number in the sequence will be 9.

Number sequences can be tricky if you are not good with numbers. You need to look out for the patterns that are linking the numbers within the sequence. How does one number get to another? What changes? You need to be able to work out what the pattern is, in order to successfully complete the question.

Find the Missing Word

Work out what word is missing in order to complete the sentence.

Example:

Mountain is to climb as slope is to...

How to work it out:

- You need to work out how the words are linked.

- For example, you climb a mountain, so you would ski on a slope. Therefore the correct answer would be ski.

Brush up on your vocabulary and gain a greater understanding of word meanings!

For these types of questions, it is important to have a good understanding of vocabulary. This can significantly improve your score in regards to Reasoning.

Antonyms / Synonyms

Work out what word means the opposite or the same as the word stated.

Example:

Rich is the antonym of ...

How to work out the antonym:

- Antonym means opposite, so you need to find a word that means the opposite to 'rich', which would be 'poor'.

How to work out the synonym:

- To work out the synonym for the same example, you need to find a word that means 'the same as'.

- Therefore a word meaning the same as 'rich' could be 'wealthy'.

REASONING -
TEST 1

(You have 9 minutes in which to complete the 30 questions).

Question 1

Dog is to canine as wolf is to...

A	B	C	D
Vulture	Lupine	Piscine	Bovine

Question 2

Rose is to flower as...

A	B	C	D
Petal is to flower	Root is to tree	Palm is to tree	Seeds is to tree

Question 3

Belinda studies for 5 hours and 12 minutes and Sheila studies for 314 minutes. *Who works for the longest period of time?*

A	B
Belinda	Sheila

Question 4

Paper is to timber as _ _ _ _ _ _ _ is to hide.

A	B	C	D
Leather	Ox	Animal	Seek

Question 5

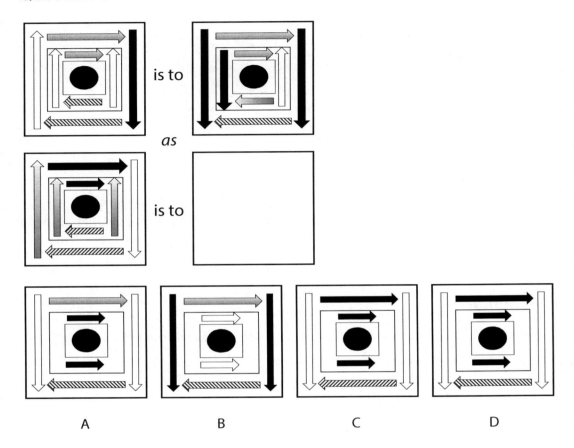

Answer

Question 6

which of the below figures will have you left?

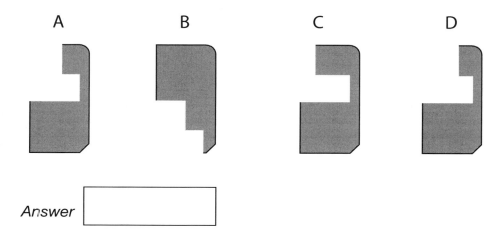

Answer

Question 7

Consider this number sequence:

$$3 \quad 5 \quad 9 \quad 11 \quad 15$$

Which of the following comes next?

A	B	C	D
19	17	20	18

Question 8

Consider the sequence of shapes.

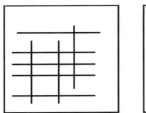 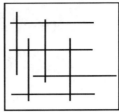 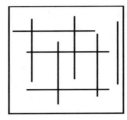

What comes next in the sequence?

| A | B | C | D |

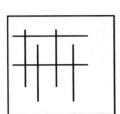 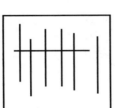 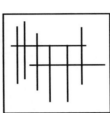 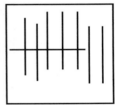

Answer

Question 9

Unprecedented means the same as…

A	B	C	D
Extraordinary	Common	Bad	Standard

Question 10

Work out which option fits best in the missing square in order to complete the sequence.

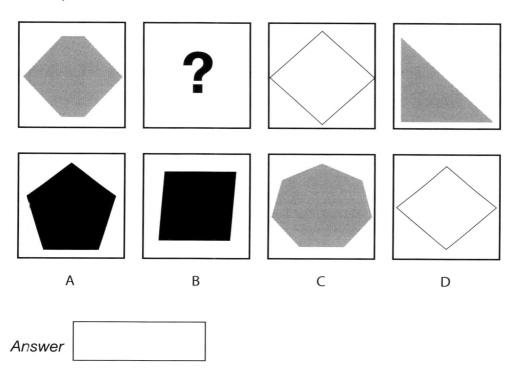

A   B   C   D

Answer

Question 11

Take a look at the following row of numbers.

2, 8, 14, 20, 26, 32, ?

Which number comes next from the options available?

A	B	C	D
36	42	38	48

Question 12

Work out which option fits best in the missing square in order to complete the sequence.

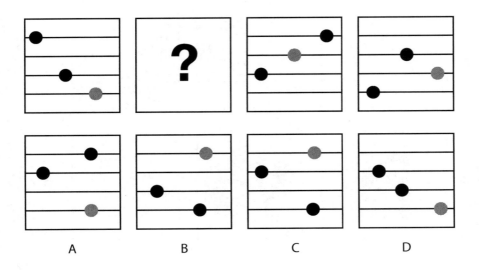

| A | B | C | D |

Answer [   ]

Question 13

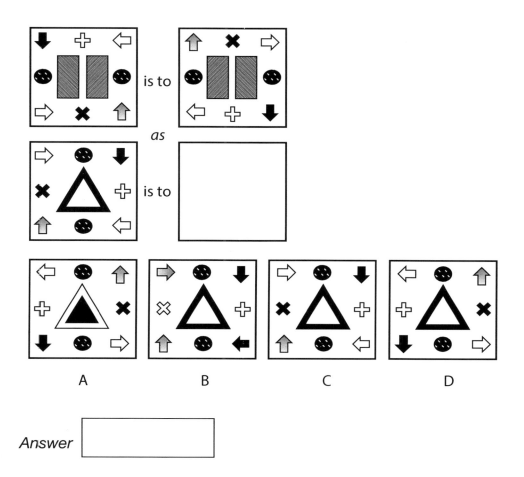

A   B   C   D

Answer

Question 14

Futile means the same as...

A	B	C	D
Modest	Angry	Sad	Pointless

Question 15

Mirror is to reflect as sun is to…

A	B	C	D
Shine	Hot	Baking	Bright

Question 16

Fill in the missing blank in order to complete the sequence.

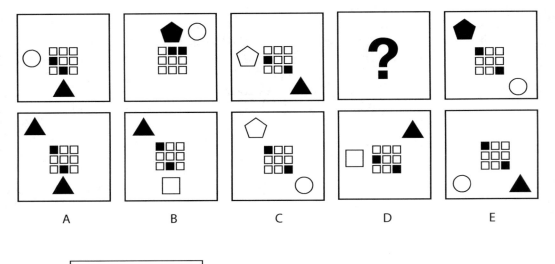

A   B   C   D   E

Answer

Question 17

Fill in the missing blank in order to complete the sequence.

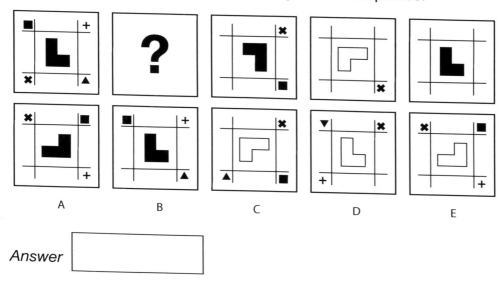

A   B   C   D   E

Answer

Question 18

Consider the following sequence.

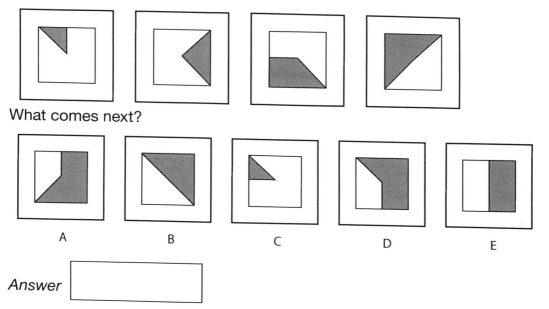

What comes next?

A   B   C   D   E

Answer

Question 19

Take a look at the following row of numbers. Which number comes next from the options available?

76, 2, 64, 8, ?, 14, 40, 20, 28

A	B	C	D	E
50	52	16	42	20

Question 20

Take a look at the following row of numbers. Which number comes next from the options available?

3, 9, ?, 81, 243, 729, 2187

A	B	C	D	E
44	27	18	59	32

Question 21

Superficial is closest in meaning to...

A	B	C	D	E
Authentic	Genuine	Exterior	Interior	Thoughtful

Question 22

What figure comes next in the series?

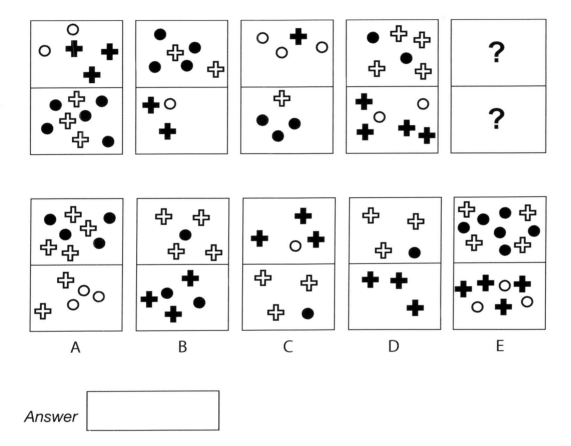

A   B   C   D   E

Answer

Question 23

Deny is to grant as…

A	B	C	D
Kill is to live	Day is to night	Love is to lust	Justice is to law

Question 24

What comes next in the series?

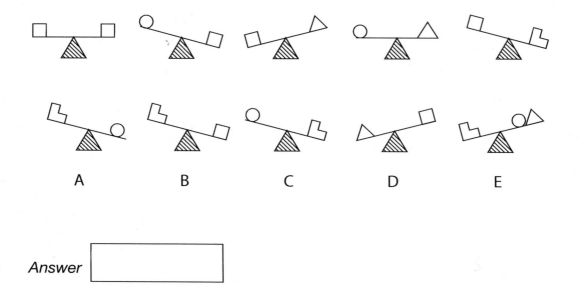

A   B   C   D   E

Answer

Question 25

Jason watches twice as much TV as John. Mark watches half the amount of TV as John. Who watches the least amount of television?

A	B	C	D
John	Mark	Jason	Cannot be determined

Question 26

Placid is the opposite to…

A	B	C	D
Imperturbable	Clamorous	Docile	Serene

Question 27

What comes next in the sequence?

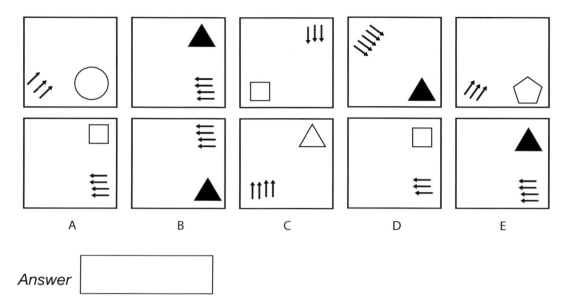

| A | B | C | D | E |

Answer

Question 28

Which of the following words contains the most vowels?

A	B	C	D
Tenacious	Collaborate	Between	Audaciously

Question 29

Billy walks for 1400 metres whilst Sam walks for 1.4 kilometres.

Who walks the furthest?

A	B	C
Billy	Sam	Both the same

Question 30

Consider the sequence of shapes.

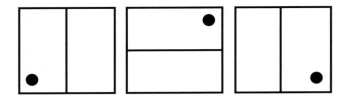

Which of the following shapes comes next in the sequence?

A	B	C	D	E

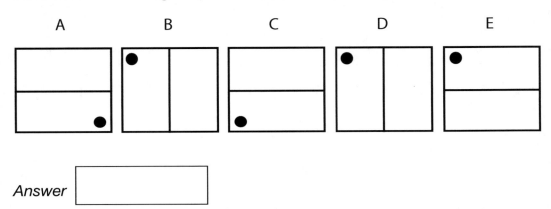

Answer

ANSWERS TO REASONING – TEST SECTION 1

Q1. B = lupine

EXPLANATION = lupine can be defined as "relating to the characteristics of wolves"; just like canine can be defined as "relating to the characteristics of dogs".

Q2. C = palm is to tree

EXPLANATION = rose is to flower as palm is to tree.

Q3. B = Sheila

EXPLANATION = Belinda works for 5 hours and 12 minutes (or in minutes, she works 312 minutes). Sheila works for 314 minutes (or in hours and minutes, she works 5 hours and 14 minutes). Therefore, Sheila works the most hours.

Q4. A = leather

EXPLANATION = paper is made from timber, and leather is made from hide.

Q5. C

EXPLANATION = Within the top two squares the arrows pointing to the right are grey, arrows pointing to the left have diagonal stripes pointing from top left to bottom right, arrows pointing down are black, and arrows pointing up are white. Within the bottom two squares, the arrows pointing to the right are black, the arrows pointing to the left have diagonal stripes from bottom left to top right, the arrows pointing down are white, and the arrows pointing up are grey.

Q6. C

EXPLANATION = if you rotated the rectangular figure 90° clockwise, you will see that the shape missing in the top left corner is the same shape taken from the question.

Q7. B = 17

EXPLANATION = the number sequence follows the pattern of: plus 2, plus 4, plus 2, plus 4 and so forth. Therefore, we need to add 2 to the final number in the sequence. 15+2=17.

Q8. C

EXPLANATION = the vertical lines are increasing by 1 each time throughout the sequence, and the horizontal lines are decreasing by 1 each time.

Q9. A = Extraordinary

EXPLANATION = Extraordinary can be defined as 'something that is very unusual or remarkable'.

Q10. A

EXPLANATION = the sequence is deducting one side from the previous shape. Also, the colour pattern alternates from grey, to black, to white. For example, the square has 4 sides, which then becomes a triangle with 3 sides.

Q11. C = 38

EXPLANATION = the numbers are following the pattern of adding 6 each time.

Q12. C

EXPLANATION = as the sequence progresses, the dots move down one line each time, once the dot reaches the bottom it goes back to the top.

Q13. A

Rule 1 = in the top set of squares each shape is either the same colour, shade or pattern. For example, arrows pointing down and the multiplication symbols are black, arrows pointing either left or right are white and circles are chequered etc.

Rule 2 = the only difference between the items in the left square and the right square are that each symbol swaps sides or corner.

Rule 3 = in the first square, the black arrow pointing downwards in the top left hand corner is now in the bottom right hand corner of the right square etc.

Q14. D = pointless

EXPLANATION = futile means "incapable of producing any useful result, i.e. pointless".

Q15. A = shine

EXPLANATION = mirror is to reflect, as sun is to shine.

Q16. B

Rule 1 = The position of the large shape is determined by the small, black squares.

Rule 2 = for the large shapes; one shape has to be white, and the other has to be black.

Figure A can be ruled out because both of the large shapes are black, and one of them should be white. Figure C can be ruled out because both of the large shapes are white, and one of them should be black. Figure D can be ruled out because the black triangle should be positioned in the bottom right corner. Figure E can be ruled out because the white circle should be positioned in the top left corner.

Q17. E

Rule 1 = the shape in the middle rotates 90° anti-clockwise as the sequence progresses. The shape in the middle alternates from black to white as the sequence progresses.

Rule 2 = the small shapes move one position to the next corner (in a clockwise manner).

Rule 3 = as the shapes rotate around, a shape is left off. You will notice, that the 'cross' shape appears the most, therefore this must be the beginning of this sequence, and so the last shape rotated (using the 'cross' to begin) will be left off.

Figure A can be ruled out because the shape in the middle needs to be white, not black. Figure B can be ruled out because the shape in the middle needs to be white, and rotated 90° anti-clockwise. Also, the small shapes do not follow the correct pattern. Figure C can be ruled out because the shape in the middle needs to be rotated 180°. Also the small shapes do not follow the correct pattern. Figure D can be ruled out because the shape in the middle needs to be rotated 90° anti-clockwise. None of the small shapes are in the correct position.

Q18. D

EXPLANATION = the large triangle is rotated 90° clockwise as the sequence progresses. It then adds the small triangle (at the start of the sequence) to fill in the gap, and therefore the correct answer would be answer option D.

Q19. B = 52

EXPLANATION = all of the odd numbers are decreasing by 12, and all of the even numbers are increasing by 6.

Q20. B = 27

EXPLANATION = each number is multiplied by 3 as the sequence progresses. Therefore, 9 needs to be multiplied by 3 = 27.

Q21. C = exterior

EXPLANATION = superficial means "existing or occurring at or on the surface" (external). Therefore, the closest in meaning is exterior.

Q22. C

Rule 1 = in the top half of the first box, and using a zig-zag method across the sequence, it contains 3 black crosses and 2 white dots, this decreases by 1 each time, until it reaches the end whereby the sequence starts again.

Rule 2 = in the bottom half of the first box, and using a zig-zag method across the sequence, it contains 3 white crosses and 5 black dots. This decreases by 1 each time, until it reaches the end whereby the sequence starts again.

Figure A can be ruled out because the top half of the box should contain 3 black crosses and 1 white dot. The bottom half of the box should contain 3 white crosses and 1 black dot. Figure B can be ruled out because the colours and number of shapes in each half of the box is incorrect. Figure D can be ruled out because the top half of the box should have 3 black crosses, not 3 white crosses. The bottom half of the box should contain a white dot. Figure E can be ruled out because the top box should contain 3 black crosses and 1 black dot; and the bottom half of the box should contain 3 white crosses and a black dot.

Q23. B = day is to night

EXPLANATION = deny is to grant as day is to night.

Q24. C

Rule 1 = squares weigh more than the circles.

Rule 2 = squares weigh more than the triangles.

Rule 3 = triangles and circles weigh the same.

Rule 3 = 'L' shapes weigh more than the squares.

Figure A can be ruled out because the 'L' shape weighs more than circles, therefore the scales are not correct. Figure B can be ruled out because the 'L' shape weighs more than squares; and therefore the scales are incorrect. Figure D can be ruled out because squares weigh more than triangles. Figure E can be ruled out because you are not given any indication as to whether the circle and the triangle would weigh more than the 'L' shape.

Q25. B = Mark

EXPLANATION = Jason watches double the amount of John. Mark watches ½ the amount of John. Therefore, Mark must watch the least amount of television.

Q26. B = clamorous

EXPLANATION = the meaning of placid is "not easily upset or excited". Imperturbable, serene and docile are all synonyms of the word 'placid' (i.e. meaning the same), therefore the opposite in meaning is clamorous, a word used to describe a loud or confusing noise.

Q27. E

Rule 1 = the arrows move one point anti-clockwise as the sequence progresses.

Rule 2 = the arrows point to the corner in which the next shape should be positioned.

Rule 3 = the number of arrows determine how many sides the next shape should contain.

Rule 4 = the shapes alternate from white to black.

Figure A can be ruled out because a black triangle should be in the position of the white square. Figure B can be ruled out because the black triangle should be in the top right corner; and the arrows should be in the bottom right corner. Figure C can be ruled out because the triangle should be black not white; and the arrows should be in the bottom right corner, not the bottom left corner. Figure D can be ruled out because the white square should be replaced with a black triangle.

Q28. D = audaciously

EXPLANATION = the word 'audaciously' contains six vowels. No other word, out of the answer options available, contains more vowels.

Q29. C = both the same

EXPLANATION = Billy walks for 1400 metres. To convert that into kilometres, you need to divide by 1000. So, 1400 ÷ 1000 = 1.4 kilometres. Sam walked 1.4 kilometres (to convert into metres, you need to multiply 1.4 by 1000 = 1.4 x 1000 = 1400 metres). Therefore they both walked the same distance.

Q30. E

Rule 1 = every other shape is a reflection. For example, the 3rd shape is a reflection of the 1st. Therefore the next shape in the sequence should be a reflection of the 2nd.

Rule 2 = the line in the middle of the square rotates 90° as the sequence progresses.

Therefore, the next shape in the sequence needs to contain a horizontal line, with the black dot positioned in the top left corner of the square.

REASONING -
TEST 2

(You have 9 minutes in which to complete the 30 questions).

Question 1

Consider the following sequence.

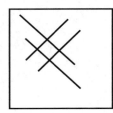 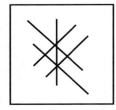 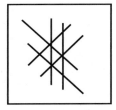

Which of the following comes next in the sequence?

 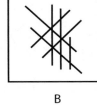 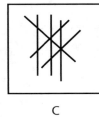 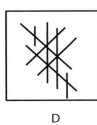 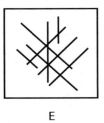

A   B   C   D   E

Answer

Question 2

What comes next in the sequence?

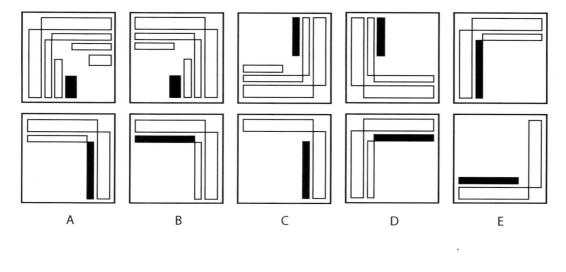

A	B	C	D	E

Answer

Question 3

Crouch is to stand, as devastating is to…

A	B	C	D
Damaging	Cataclysmic	Beneficial	Upset

Question 4

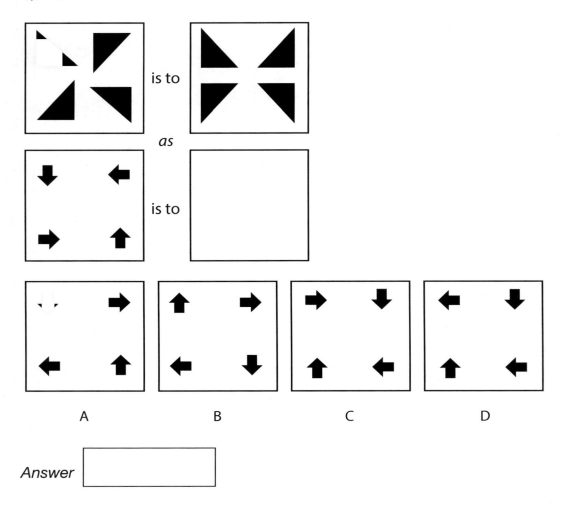

A   B   C   D

Answer

Question 5

Condense means the same as...

A	B	C	D
Expand	Compress	Lengthen	Express

Question 6

Alleviate is to irritate as disagreeable is to...

A	B	C	D
Repulsion	Pleasant	Nastiness	Different

Question 7

Consider the sequence of shapes.

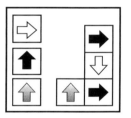 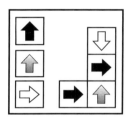 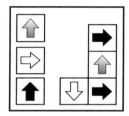 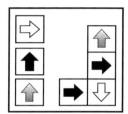

What comes next in the sequence?

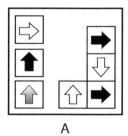 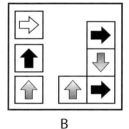 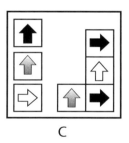 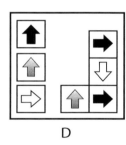

| A | B | C | D |

Answer

Question 8

Take a look at the following row of numbers. Which number comes next from the options available?

110, 14, 104, 15, 98, 16, ?

A	B	C	D
92	17	90	111

Question 9

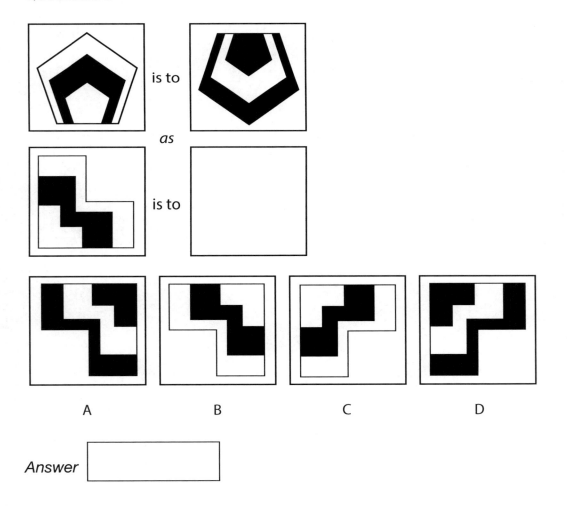

A   B   C   D

Answer

Question 10

Consider the sequence of the shapes.

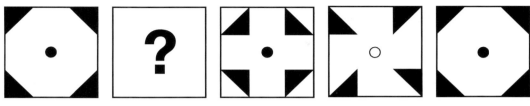

What shape fills in the missing blank in order to complete the sequence?

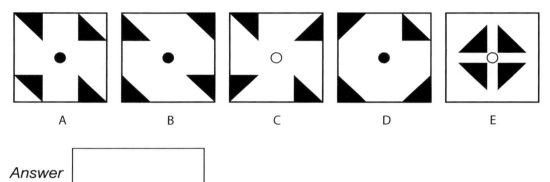

| A | B | C | D | E |

Answer [   ]

Question 11

Rebuke is to reprimand as contingent is to…

A	B	C	D
Fortuitous	Deliberate	Idyllic	Honourable

Question 12

Crow is to chick as tiger is to…

A	B	C	D
Pup	Infant	Ape	Cub

Question 13

Eminent is to unknown as descendant is to…

A	B	C	D
Accent	Ancestor	Family	Friend

Question 14

Consider the following sequence.

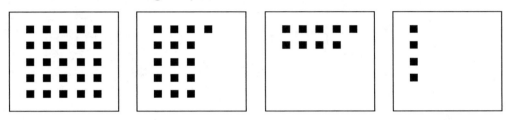

What comes next in the sequence?

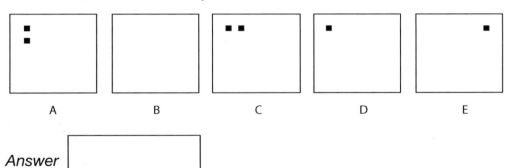

| A | B | C | D | E |

Answer

Question 15

Take a look at the following row of numbers. Which numbers complete the sequence?

?   115   100   85   70   ?

A	B	C	D	E
145 and 60	130 and 55	100 and 60	110 and 100	150 and 35

Question 16

Bull is to herd as gorilla is to...

A	B	C	D	E
Banana	Monkey	Human	Band	Group

Question 17

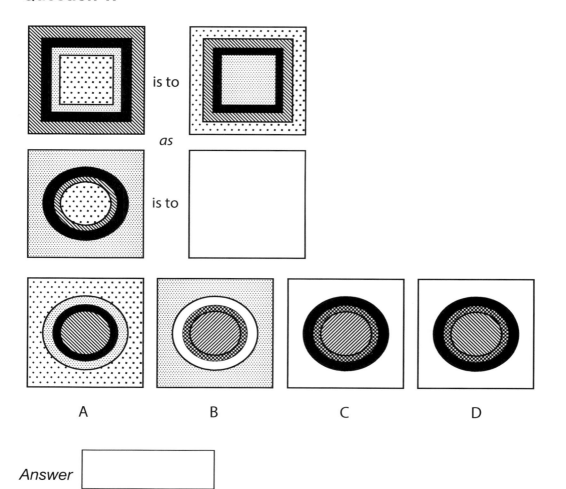

is to

as

is to

A   B   C   D

Answer

Question 18

Consider the following sequence.

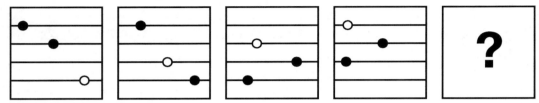

What shape fills in the missing blank in order to complete the sequence?

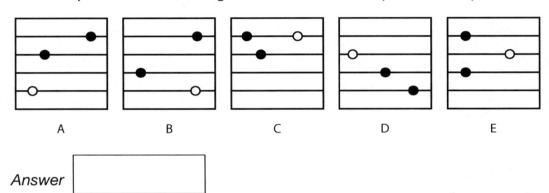

| A | B | C | D | E |

Answer

Question 19

Rodney spends £7.45 at the shop whilst Billy spends 459 pence.

Who spends the least amount of money?

A	B
Rodney	Billy

Question 20

Hannah can run faster than Michael. Michael can run faster than David who is slower than Peter. Peter is faster than Hannah.

Who is the slowest?

A	B	C	D	E
Hannah	Michael	David	Peter	Cannot say

Question 21

Brenda slept for 6 hours and Elizabeth slept 362 minutes.

Who slept for the longest time?

A	B
Brenda	Elizabeth

Question 22

What number completes the sequence?

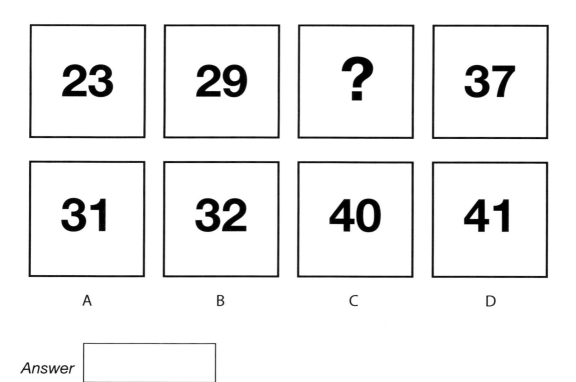

23	29	?	37

31	32	40	41
A	B	C	D

Answer [ ]

Question 23

Consider the following sequence.

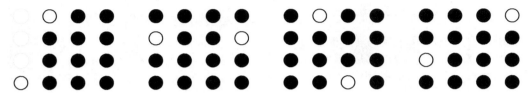

What comes next in the sequence?

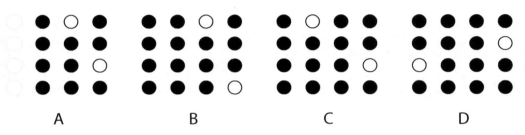

| A | B | C | D |

Answer

Question 24

Acumen is the same as…

A	B	C	D
Witlessness	Diversity	Valiant	Astuteness

Question 25

Consider the following sequence.

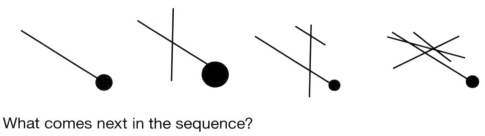

What comes next in the sequence?

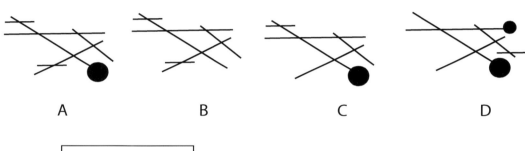

| A | B | C | D |

Answer

Question 26

Take a look at the following row of numbers. Which number comes next from the options available?

10, 5, 8, 6, 6, 7, 4, ?

A	B	C	D	E
0	2	8	9	12

Question 27

Consider the following sequence.

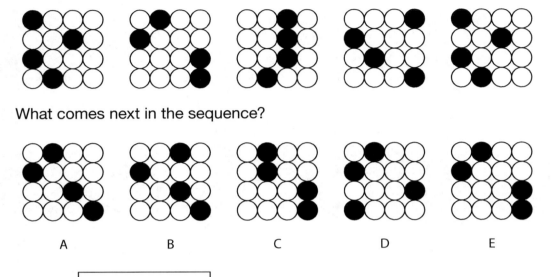

What comes next in the sequence?

A   B   C   D   E

Answer

Question 28

Ecstatic is the opposite of...

A	B	C	D	E
Thrilled	Adaptable	Bouncy	Disconsolate	Divergent

Question 29

Narcissistic is the same as...

A	B	C	D	E
Cowardly	Conceited	Bold	Dynamic	Adventurous

Question 30

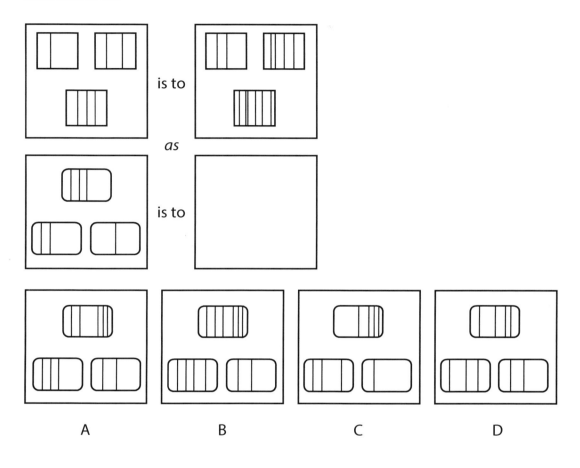

A   B   C   D

Answer

ANSWERS TO REASONING – TEST SECTION 2

Q1. B

EXPLANATION = the sequence follows the pattern of adding one vertical line as the sequence progresses. For example, the first shape contains no vertical lines, the second box contains one vertical line, and the third box contains two vertical lines. Therefore the next shape in the sequence must contain three vertical lines.

Q2. C

Rule 1 = the figure rotates 90° clockwise as the sequence progresses.

Rule 2 = as the sequence progresses, the black shape switches sides.

Rule 3 = the shaded shape disappears in the next box; and the shape closest to the middle becomes the shaded shape.

Figure A can be ruled out because the small horizontal rectangle should have disappeared. Figure B can be ruled out because the shaded shape should be a small vertical rectangle, not a small horizontal rectangle. Figure D can be ruled out because the figure has been rotated the wrong way; and the black shape should be a vertical rectangle, not a horizontal rectangle. Figure E can be ruled out because the figure has been rotated the wrong way. The shaded rectangle should also be vertical, not horizontal.

Q3. C = beneficial

EXPLANATION = crouch is to stand as devastating is to beneficial.

Q4. A

EXPLANATION = within the top set of squares, the top left and bottom right shapes remain in the same position. The bottom left and top right shapes rotate 180°.

Q5. B = Compress

EXPLANATION = condense means 'to contain or make smaller'. i.e. 'the morning session was condensed into a half hour package', and compress means to 'squeeze, or make smaller'.

Q6. B = pleasant

EXPLANATION = alleviate is to irritate as disagreeable is to pleasant.

Q7. D
EXPLANATION = within each square of the series, the 3 squares to the left move up one space as the sequence progresses. The 4 squares to the right move up one space as the sequence progresses.

Q8. A
EXPLANATION = All odd numbers are decreasing by 6 each time and all even numbers are increasing by 1.

Q9. D
EXPLANATION = the colour pattern alternates from black to white. The shape is flipped horizontally from box 1 to box 2. Therefore you need to do the same to box 3, to get box 4.

Q10. C
Rule 1 = each shaded triangle has been rotated 90° clockwise.

Rule 2 = the dot in the centre of the shape alternates between black and white.

Figure C is the only figure that fits in with the sequence. None of the other figures work in the sequence.

Q11. A = Fortuitous
EXPLANATION = Rebuke is to reprimand as contingent is to fortuitous.

Q12. D = cub
EXPLANATION = a baby crow is called a chick, and a baby tiger is called a cub.

Q13. B = ancestor
EXPLANATION = eminent is to unknown as descendant is to ancestor.

Q14. D
Rule 1 = the shapes rotate 90° clockwise as the sequence progresses.

Rule 2 = from box 1 to box 2, 9 squares from the far right (vertical) side are taken off. From box 2 to box 3, 7 squares are taken. From box 3 to box 4, 5 squares are taken.

Rule 3 = so, the next box will have 3 squares taken.

Q15. B = 130 and 55

EXPLANATION = all the numbers are decreasing by 15 each time.

Q16. D = band

EXPLANATION = a group of bull's form a 'herd', just as a group of gorillas are a 'band' of gorillas.

Q17. A

Within the top left-hand square the different coloured/shaded squares work from the outside towards the centre. Within the top right-hand square the different coloured/shaded squares work from the centre towards the outside.

Q18. A

Rule 1 = the two black dots remain straight after one another (there is no line in between the two black dots).

Rule 2 = the white dot remains one line ahead of the last black dot.

Rule 3 = the dots move up one line each time.

Figure B can be ruled out because the black dots should not have a line in between them. Figure C can be ruled out because the black dot should not be on the same line as the white dot. Figure D can be ruled out because the white dot needs to be on the bottom line. Figure E can be ruled out because the two black dots have been separated by the white dot in the middle.

Q19. B = Billy

EXPLANATION = Rodney spends £7.45, which is equivalent to 745 pence. Billy spends 459 pence, which is equivalent to £4.59. Therefore the person who spent the least amount of money is Billy.

Q20. C = David

EXPLANATION = Peter is faster than Hannah, and Hannah can run faster than Michael. Michael can run faster than David, and David is slower than Peter. Therefore, the slowest runner is David.

Q21. B = Elizabeth

EXPLANATION = Brenda slept for 6 hours, which is equivalent to 360 minutes. Elizabeth slept for 362, which is equivalent to 6 hours and 2 minutes, therefore Elizabeth slept for the longest time.

Q22. A

Rule 1 = the sequence contains prime numbers in order (a prime number is a number which only multiplies by 1 and itself).

Figure B can be ruled out because 32 is not a prime number; the numbers 1, 2, 4, 8 16 and 32 all go into 32. Figure C can be ruled out because 40 is not a prime number; the numbers 1, 2, 4, 5, 8, 10, 20 and 40 all go into 40. Figure D can be ruled out because, and although 41 is a prime number, it does not fit in the third box within the sequence.

Q23. C

Rule 1 = The white dot which starts in the bottom left corner, moves two places clockwise around the edge of the figure.

Rule 2 = the white dot which starts on the second left of the top row, moves three places clockwise around the edge of the figure.

Figure A can be ruled out because the white dot third on the first row should be the second dot on the first row. Figure B can be ruled out because the white dot in the bottom right corner should be one place above it; the white dot on the first row should also be moved one place anti-clockwise. Figure D can be ruled out because the white dot on the third row should be the second dot on the first row. Also, the white dot on the second row should be moved one place clockwise.

Q24. D = Astuteness

EXPLANATION = acumen can be defined 'as the ability to make good judgements'. Therefore the closest in meaning to acumen is astuteness.

Q25. C

EXPLANATION = another line is added to the shape as the sequence progresses. The last shape in the sequence shows four lines, so the next shape in the sequence must contain five lines.

Q26. C

Rule 1=Every 1st number decreases by 2 each time, for example, '10, 8, 6, 4'

Rule 2=Every 2nd number increases by 1 each time, for example, '5, 6, 7...'

EXPLANATION: The next number in the sequence would be the penultimate number, 7, plus 1. Therefore the answer is C=8.

Q27. E

Rule 1 = on the first row, the black dot moves one space, left to right.

Rule 2 = on the second row, the black dot moves two spaces, right to left.

Rule 3 = on the third row, the black dot moves three spaces, left to right.

Rule 4 = on the fourth row, the black dot moves two spaces, left to right.

Figure A can be ruled out because the black dot on the third row should be the last dot on that row. Figure B can be ruled out because the black dot on the first row should be the second dot, not the third dot. Also, the black dot on the third row should be the last dot on that row. Figure C can be ruled out because the black dot on the second row should be the first dot, not the second. Figure D can be ruled out because the black dot on the last row should be the last dot, not the first dot.

Q28. D = Disconsolate

EXPLANATION = ecstatic means 'feeling or expressing overwhelming happiness.' Therefore the opposite of this is disconsolate, which is defined as 'being very unhappy or sad'.

Q29. B = conceited

EXPLANATION = narcissistic means "the pursuit of gratification from vanity or egotistic admiration of oneself". Therefore the closest in meaning out of the options is 'conceited', which means being arrogant and egotistical.

Q30. B

EXPLANATION = within the first set of shapes the corresponding lines within each square are doubling each time.

ROYAL NAVY RECRUITING TEST –
VERBAL ABILITY

As part of your Royal Navy Recruiting test, you will be required to take a Verbal Ability test.

Verbal Ability is a test used to assess a candidate's ability to recognise relationships between words and sentences. Typical questions in relation to Verbal Ability include completing the sentence, rephrasing sentences, grouping words, word discrepancies and so forth. All these question types are used to determine how well a candidate can quickly and effectively work through verbal formats, and demonstrate high levels of literary and verbal understanding.

On the day of your RN assessment, **you will have 9 minutes in which to answer 30 questions** relating to Verbal Ability. In your real test, please note that you will be given a separate sheet of paper, on which you would write your answers. For the purpose of the book, it would be a useful tool to write down your answers on a piece of paper, or use a highlighter to indicate your choice.

In order to gain some understanding of the types of questions you will face during this sub-test, and how you go about answering them, check out the following pages of example questions. These examples provide clear and detailed descriptions of how to answer the question correctly, what to expect, what to look out for, and useful tips regarding each question type.

Good luck.

EXAMPLES OF
VERBAL ABILITY

Complete the Sentence

The following sentence has one word missing. Which ONE word can be inserted into the sentence, so that it makes the best sense?

Example:

The man took his dog for a _ _ _ _ _ _ _ walk.

A – Bored

B – Daily

C – Funny

D – Suddenly

E – Running

How to work it out:

- You need to work out which word, out of the answer options available, fits in with the structure of the sentence.

- Pay attention to past, present and future tenses.

- Pay attention to spelling!

- Pay attention to whether or not the sentence makes sense after adding in the new word.

Answer:

B = Daily

For these types of questions, you need to find a word that would fit in with the structure of the sentence. Pay attention to how the sentence is written. For example, is it written in past, present or future tense? This will help you to eliminate some of the word choices.

Pay attention to tense, i.e. is the sentence written in past, present or future?

The sentence needs to be grammatically correct. If it helps, read out the sentence once you have chosen the word to see whether or not the sentence reads correctly.

Odd One Out

Identify which word is the odd one out.

Example:

A – Sword
B – Dagger
C – Arrow
D – Spear
E – Shield

How to work it out:

- Pay attention to how the words can be linked and relate to one another.

In the above example, you should be able to notice that sword, dagger, arrow and spear are all types of weapon. A shield is a protective instrument, and therefore is the odd one out.

Answer:

Shield

For these types of questions, you need to work out how the words are linked, and from that, which word is the odd one out.

These questions are relatively straightforward if you can spot the link between the words.

Pay attention to word meanings and relationships. How are the words related to one another?

Word Jumbles

In the sentence, the word outside the brackets will only go with three of the words inside the brackets, in order to form a longer word. Which ONE word will it NOT go with?

Example:

Down

A	B	C	D
(Out)	(Size)	(Ward)	(Load)

How to work it out:

- You need to work out whether or not the word outside the bracket, in this case (down), can make a new word with the word inside the bracket.
- So, downsize can be made.
- Downward can be made.
- Download can be made.
- Downout is not a word, and therefore option A does not work.

Answer:

A = Out

> **It would help to have a good knowledge of vocabulary! Brush up on your words!**

The key to remember for these types of questions is that once you join the words together, they have to read as one word (not as two).

Connect the Words

In each question there are two pairs of words. Only one of the answers will go equally well with both pairs of words. Work out which answer best relates with the given words.

(Look out for meanings of the words and other possibilities of how another word could be used in that situation).

Example:

(fall   tumble)   (journey   outing)

A	B	C	D
(Travel)	(Trip)	(Trap)	(Drop)

How to work it out:

- You need to work out how the two brackets of words can be linked.
- You need to find a word that has a relationship with both the words in the first bracket, and both the words in the second bracket.
- Travel would not be appropriate because it doesn't fit with the first set of words.
- Trap doesn't work because it doesn't fit with the second set of words.
- Drop doesn't work because it doesn't fit with the second set of words.

Answer:

B – Trip (meaning to 'fall' or 'stumble' and can also mean taking a 'trip/vacation' somewhere).

> **Pay attention to how a word could be seen to have multiple meanings!**

These questions are relatively straightforward. You need to determine which answer can link both brackets of words.

A lot of words in the English language often have multiple meanings. In the above example, the word 'trip' can be used to describe someone who 'tripped over', or can be used to describe 'a journey', i.e. taking a trip somewhere.

Word Pairs

In each question there are two words. Work out which word pair relates best with the word pair shown.

Example:

Music : Sound

A	B	C	D
Vibes / tone	Loud / noisy	Listen / loud	Tone / loud

How to work it out:

- You need to work out how the two words can be related to another two words.

- You need to find the words that have a relationship with both the words shown.

For the above example, music and sound can closely be linked to vibes and tones. Music has tones and a vibe; and so does sound; and therefore this is the closest relationship in terms of meaning.

Answer:

A = vibes and tone

These questions are similar to the previous sets of questions, whereby it asks you to link the words with other words. In the above example, the words *music* and *sound* can be linked to all of the answer options in some way, but you need to find the word choice that has the best connection.

Pay attention to how both words can be closely linked to another pair of words.

Word Families

In each question, there are four or five words, your job is to pick out the word that links all the other words together.

Example:

A	B	C	D
Trousers	Clothing	Shirt	Skirt

How to work it out:

- You need to work out which word can group all of the other words to form a word family.

For the above example, 'clothing' is the word that links trousers, skirt and shirt, so therefore the correct answer would be B.

Answer:

B = clothing

Antonyms / Synonyms

Work out what word means the opposite or the same as the word stated.

Example:

Beautiful

How to work out the antonym:

- Antonym means opposite, so you need to find a word that means the opposite to beautiful. For example, ugly.

How to work out the synonym:

- To work out the synonym for the same example, you need to find a word that means 'the same as'. For example, stunning.

VERBAL ABILITY -
TEST 1

(You have 9 minutes in which to complete the 30 questions).

Question 1

What word pair shown has the most similar relationship to...

Colour : Spectrum

A	B	C	D
Verse : Rhyme	Waves : Sound	Tone : Scale	Nature : Atmosphere

Question 2

Which one word has a meaning that extends to or includes the meaning of all the other words?

A	B	C	D	E
Gymnastics	Swimming	Running	Training	Football

Question 3

Which of the following is the odd one out?

A	B	C	D	E
Mallet	Sledgehammer	Ball Peen	Lump Hammer	Hatchet

Question 4

Which word does not have a similar meaning to – imaginary?

A	B	C	D
Apocryphal	Fictional	Figmental	Fickle

Question 5

Which word does not have a similar meaning to – result?

A	B	C	D
Outcome	Effect	Upshot	Affect

Question 6

In the line below, the word outside of the brackets will only go with three of the words inside the brackets to make longer words. Which ONE word will it NOT go with?

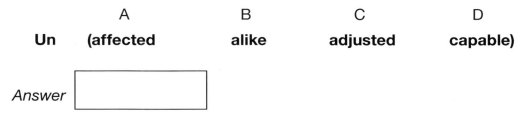

	A	B	C	D
Un	(affected	alike	adjusted	capable)

Answer

Question 7

Which of the following words is the odd one out?

A	B	C	D	E
Bird	Dog	Helicopter	Plane	Cloud

Question 8

Which word is the odd one out?

A	B	C	D	E
London	Paris	Lisbon	Prague	Nuremberg

Question 9

Which word is the odd one out?

A	B	C	D	E
Ostrich	Parrots	Penguins	Dodo	Owls

Question 10

In the line below, the word outside of the brackets will only go with three of the words inside the brackets to make longer words. Which one word will it not go with?

	A	B	C	D
Un	**(assuming**	**admired**	**usual**	**draught)**

Answer

Question 11

Four of the five sentences have the same meaning. Which one sentence has a different meaning?

A – Mike spent £180 during his shopping trip.
B – During his shopping trip, Mike spent £180.
C – The shopping trip cost Mike £180.
D – Mike made £180 from his shopping trip.
E – A total of £180 was spent on Mikes shopping trip.

Answer

Question 12

In the line below, the word outside of the brackets will only go with three of the words inside the brackets to make longer words. Which one word will it not go with?

	A	B	C	D
An	**(tarctic**	**aerobic**	**ability**	**droid)**

Answer

Question 13

Which word is the odd one out?

A	B	C	D	E
Hungry	Ravenous	Famished	Esurient	Replete

Question 14

Fill in the missing word so the sentence reads correctly.

I _ _ _ _ _ _ _ that good things come to those who wait.

A	B	C	D
Belief	Be leave	Believing	Believe

Question 15

Fill in the missing word so the sentence reads correctly.

_ _ _ _ _ _ _ going to be in big trouble when they get home.

A	B	C	D
Thair	There	Their	They're

Question 16

In the line below, the word outside of the brackets will only go with three of the words inside the brackets to make longer words. Which one word will it not go with?

	A	B	C	D
In	**(direct**	**famous**	**animate**	**cart)**

Answer

Question 17

Which of the following is the odd one out?

A	B	C	D
Trumpet	Violin	Harp	Guitar

Question 18

The following sentence has one word missing. Which one word makes the best sense of the sentence?

A submarine is a watercraft _ _ _ _ _ _ _ of independent operation underwater.

A	B	C	D	E
Evolved	Built	Capable	Designed	Submersible

Question 19

Read the following statement, then choose the correct answer from the choices available.

Sam is Peter's mother's brother and Adam is Peter's father's father. John is Adam's son.

A – Adam is Peter's grandfather.

B – Sam is Peter's nephew.

C – Adam and John are brothers.

D – Adam is Peter's uncle.

Answer

Question 20

Four of the five sentences have the same meaning. Which one sentence has a different meaning?

A – It was a little girl who was pushed over by a tall boy.
B – The tall boy pushed over a little girl.
C – The little girl pushed over the boy.
D – The little girl fell over as a result of being pushed by the tall boy.
E – The tall boy got into trouble for pushing over a little girl.

Answer

Question 21

In the line below, the word outside of the brackets will only go with three of the words inside the brackets to make longer words. Which one word will it not go with?

	A	B	C	D
Im	**(migrate**	**practical**	**pose**	**closure)**

Answer

Question 22

The following sentence has one word missing. Which one word makes the best sense of the sentence?

The man _ _ _ _ _ _ _ he wanted to go home.

A	B	C	D	E
Chose	Needed	Decided	Ran	Boasted

Question 23

The following sentence has one word missing. Which one word makes the best sense of the sentence?

The weather forecaster informed the public of the _ _ _ _ _ _ _ rain.

A	B	C	D	E
Likelihood	Chance	Dry	Need	Potential

Question 24

Which of the following words is the odd one out?

A	B	C	D
Jupiter	Earth	Mars	Moon

Question 25

In the line below, the word outside of the brackets will only go with three of the words inside the brackets to make longer words. Which one word will it not go with?

	A	B	C	D
In	**(coherent**	**dulgent**	**believable**	**candescent)**

Answer

Question 26

In each question, there are two pairs of words. Only one of the answers will go equally well with both these pairs.

(Smart   clever)   (Light   sunny)

A	B	C	D
Bright	Dark	Night	Intelligent

Question 27

In the line below, the word outside of the brackets will only go with three of the words inside the brackets to make longer words. Which ONE word will it NOT go with?

	A	B	C	D
In	**(appropriate**	**justice**	**ethical**	**animate)**

Answer

Question 28

Which of the following is the odd one out?

A	B	C	D	E
Rose	Lily	Daisy	Petal	Sunflower

Question 29

Which word does not have a similar meaning to – talkative?

A	B	C	D
Garrulous	Loquacious	Affluent	Voluble

Question 30

Which words makes the best sense in the following sentence?

By the time Scarlett arrived at the disco, Peter _ _ _ _ _ _ _ .

A	B	C	D
Hadn't gone	Already left	Has already left	Had already left

ANSWERS TO VERBAL ABILITY – TEST SECTION 1

Q1. C = Tone : Scale

EXPLANATION = for this type of question, you need to work out what two words have the most similar meaning to the two words shown. Colour and spectrum both can be related to tone and scale. Colours have different tones and can be defined on a scale i.e. light and dark; just like a spectrum has a scale and tones of colours.

Q2. D = training

EXPLANATION = training is the one word that groups all the other words together. Gymnastics, swimming, running and football are all types of training exercises for an athletic sport.

Q3. E = Hatchet

EXPLANATION = Hatchet is the odd one out, because this item is an axe, whereas the other answers are all hammers.

Q4. D = Fickle

EXPLANATION = Fictional, Figmental and Apocryphal are all words which relate to 'imaginary'. 'Fickle' does not have a similar meaning.

Q5. D = Answer

EXPLANATION = outcome, effect and upshot are all words that have the same meaning as 'result', whereas affect means 'making a difference'.

Q6. D = capable

EXPLANATION = if you were to put 'un' with the words 'affected', 'alike' and 'adjusted', you would get: unaffected, unalike and unadjusted. However, if you tried to put 'un' with 'capable', it would not be grammatically correct. Instead you would need to put 'in' with capable for it to read 'incapable'; and therefore answer D does not go with the word outside the bracket.

Q7. B = dog

EXPLANATION = bird, helicopter, plane and cloud are all items that can be found in the sky, whereas dog is the odd one out because this is something that remains on the ground.

Q8. E = Nuremberg

EXPLANATION = London, Lisbon, Paris and Prague are all capital cities, whereas Nuremberg is not a city's capital.

Q9. D = Dodo

EXPLANATION = all of the other words refer to birds that are not extinct, whereas the dodo bird is a bird that is extinct and therefore makes it the odd one out.

Q10. D = draught

EXPLANATION = if you were to put 'un' with the words 'assuming, 'admired', and 'usual', you would get: unassuming, unadmired and unusual. However, if you were to put 'un' with 'draught', this would not be grammatically correct.

Q11. D – Mike made £180 from his shopping trip.

EXPLANATION = the other four sentences refer to Mike spending money, therefore answer option D (Mike made £180 from his shopping trip) means something different to the rest of the sentences.

Q12. C = ability

EXPLANATION = if were to put 'an' with 'tarctic', 'aerobic' and 'droid', you would get: Antarctic, anaerobic and android. However, if you were to put 'an' with 'ability', this would not be grammatically correct.

Q13. E = replete

EXPLANATION = hungry, famished, ravenous and esurient all mean 'being hungry'. Whereas, replete means the opposite of being hungry. Replete means "being full and complete", therefore this makes it the odd one out.

Q14. D = believe

EXPLANATION = in order to find the missing word, you need to work out the sentence structure. Is it past, present or future tense? The word that is grammatically correct for this sentence is 'believe'. So, the sentence would read 'I believe that good things come to those who wait'.

Q15. D = they're

EXPLANATION = in order to find the missing word, you need to work out the sentence structure. Is it in past tense or present tense or future tense? The word that is grammatically correct for this sentence is 'they're. So, the sentence would read 'they're (they are) going to be in big trouble when they get home'.

Q16. D = cart

EXPLANATION = indirect, infamous, inanimate. Therefore the word that does not fit is 'cart', as 'incart' is not a word.

Q17. A = trumpet

EXPLANATION = trumpet is the only instrument out of the options listed that requires you to play using your mouth. The other instruments only require you to play the instrument using your hands.

Q18. C = capable

EXPLANATION = the word that would best fit the sentence and would be grammatically correct is 'capable'. So, the sentence would read 'a submarine is a watercraft capable of independent operation underwater'.

Q19. A = Adam is Peter's grandfather

EXPLANATION = if Adam is Peter's father's father, he must be Peter's grandfather.

Q20. C = The little girl pushed over the boy.

EXPLANATION = the sentence 'the little girl pushed over the boy' has the opposite meaning of all the other sentences, therefore this sentence is the odd one out.

Q21. D = closure

EXPLANATION = if you were to put 'im' with 'migrate', 'practical' and 'pose', you would get: immigrate, impractical and impose. However, if you were to put 'im' with 'closure', this would be grammatically incorrect.

Q22. C = decided

EXPLANATION = the correct word that is needed in order for the sentence to be grammatically correct is 'decided'. So, the sentence would read 'the man decided he wanted to go home'.

Q23. E = potential

EXPLANATION = the correct word that is needed in order for the sentence to be grammatically correct is 'potential'. So, the sentence would read 'the weather forecaster informed the public of the potential rain'.

Q24. D = moon

EXPLANATION = the 'moon' is the odd one out because all of the other words refer to planets.

Q25. C = believable

EXPLANATION = if you were to put 'in' with the words 'coherent', 'dulgent' and 'candescent', you would get: incoherent, indulgent and incandescent. However, if you tried to put 'in' with 'believable', this would be grammatically incorrect.

Q26. A = bright

EXPLANATION = 'smart' and 'clever' can mean someone who is 'bright' or 'intelligent'. Light and sunny can also mean 'bright'.

Q27. C = ethical

EXPLANATION = if you were to put the word 'in' with the words 'appropriate', 'justice' and 'animate', you would get: inappropriate, injustice and inanimate. Therefore the word that 'in' does not go into is 'ethical'.

Q28. D = petal

EXPLANATION = 'petal' is the odd one out because all of the other words refer to 'types' of flowers, whereas 'petal' is 'part' of a flower.

Q29. C = affluent

EXPLANATION = Garrulous, loquacious and voluble are all words that have the same meaning as 'talkative'. 'Affluent' refers to 'someone who has a great deal of money', and therefore is the odd one out.

Q30. D = had already left

EXPLANATION = 'had already left' would be the correct way to end this sentence. The other three answers are not grammatically correct in the context of the sentence.

VERBAL ABILITY - *TEST 2*

(You have 9 minutes in which to complete the 30 questions).

Question 1

In the line below, the word outside of the brackets will only go with three of the words inside the brackets to make longer words. Which one word will it not go with?

	A	B	C	D
In	**(doubtable**	**bred**	**breeding**	**cautiously)**

Answer

Question 2

Which two letter word can be placed in front of the following words to make a new word?

Coming   Going   Shore   Line

Answer

Question 3

Which of the following is the odd one out?

A	B	C	D
Now	Cow	Low	How

Question 4

Which word does not have a similar meaning to – smart?

A	B	C	D
Obtuse	Resourceful	Astute	Adept

Question 5

In the line below, the word outside of the brackets will only go with three of the words inside the brackets to make longer words. Which ONE word will it NOT go with?

	A	B	C	D
In	**(decisive**	**reference**	**destructible**	**convenience)**

Answer

Question 6

In the line below, the word outside of the brackets will only go with three of the words inside the brackets to make longer words. Which ONE word will it NOT go with?

	A	B	C	D
Can	**(run**	**apé**	**did**	**cellation)**

Answer

Question 7

Which of the following words is the odd one out?

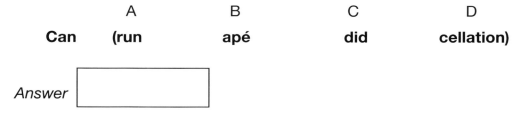

A	B	C	D	E
Swim	Run	Sprint	Sit	Walk

Question 8

In each question, there are two pairs of words. Only one of the answers will go equally well with both these pairs.

(Variety   type)   (Arrange   organise)

A	B	C	D
Sort	Tidy	Reshuffle	Move

Question 9

Which letter from the word on the left can be moved to the word on the right, to make TWO new words? The letters must not be rearranged.

(Tribal   robed)

A	B	C	D
I	B	A	L

Question 10

Which five letter word can be placed in front of the following words to make a new word?

Making   Wood   Stick   Box

Answer

Question 11

The sentence below has a word missing. Which one word makes the best sense of the sentence?

The news reporter had very little time to conduct his interview with a famous actor, so he would have to ask some _ _ _ _ _ _ _ questions in order to gather up as much information as possible.

A	B	C	D
Lengthy	Cruel	Boring	Strong

Question 12

Which of the following is the odd one out?

A	B	C	D
July	December	June	May

Question 13

Complete the following sentence.

The plan must be revised to make the project more _ _ _ _ _ _ _.

A	B	C	D
Feasable	Feasibility	Feasability	Feasible

Question 14

Which word is the odd one out?

A	B	C	D	E
Beef	Mutton	Cow	Pork	Ham

Question 15

Which word is the odd one out?

A	B	C	D	E
Anxious	Affraid	Terrified	Aghast	Fearful

Question 16

Which of the following is the odd one out?

A	B	C	D	E
Gold	Titanium	Iron	Ivory	Silver

Question 17

Which of the following sentences has a different meaning to the other four sentences?

A – On the floor lied a man who was pushed over by the bouncer.
B – The bouncer pushed a man to the floor.
C – The man was pushed to the floor by a bouncer.
D – The man was pushed by the bouncer on to the floor.
E – The bouncer was pushed by a man who then fell to the floor.

Answer

Question 18

Which two letter word can be placed in front of the following words to make a new word?

Adequate   Take   Visible   Tuition

Answer

Question 19

In the sentence below, the word outside the brackets will only go with three of the words inside the brackets in order to make a longer word. Which ONE word will it NOT go with?

	A	B	C	D
Dis	**(affirm**	**abuse**	**accord**	**cendible)**

Answer

Question 20

In the sentence below, the word outside the brackets will only go with three of the words inside the brackets in order to make a longer word. Which ONE word will it NOT go with?

	A	B	C	D
Int	**(egumentary**	**ellect**	**truments**	**elligble)**

Answer

Question 21

Which five letter word can be placed in front of the following words to make a new word?

Title   Play   View   Pose

Answer

Question 22

Which four letter word can be placed in front of the following words to make a new word?

Weight   **Wood**   **Bolt**   **Lock**

Answer

Question 23

Which four letter word can be placed in front of the following words to make a new word?

React   **Loaded**   **Cast**   **Drive**

Answer

Question 24

In each question, there are two pairs of words. Only one of the answers will go equally well with both these pairs.

(Competition   run)   (Origin   species)

A	B	C	D
Compete	Walk	Black	Race

Question 25

Which of the following dates is the odd one out?

A	B	C	D
31st June 1999	29th February 2013	29th January 2014	2nd March 2004

Question 26

Which of the following words is the odd one out?

A	B	C	D
Dragon	Dog	Fish	Donkey

Question 27

Which of the following words is the odd one out?

A	B	C	D
Thailand	Egypt	Tokyo	Vietnam

Question 28

Which of the following words is the odd one out?

A	B	C	D
Lifejacket	Mast	Stern	Anvil

Question 29

In each question, there are two pairs of words. Only one of the answers will go equally well with both these pairs.

(Tree   layer)   (Growl   woof)

A	B	C	D
Cover	Branch	Bark	Dog

Question 30

In the sentence below, the word outside the brackets will only go with three of the words inside the brackets in order to make a longer word. Which ONE word will it NOT go with?

	A	B	C	D
Rat	**(eable**	**fishes**	**reat**	**line)**

Answer [   ]

ANSWERS TO VERBAL ABILITY – TEST SECTION 2

Q1. A = doubtable

EXPLANATION = if you were to put the word 'in' with the words 'bred', 'breeding' and 'cautiously', you would make the following words; inbred, inbreeding and incautiously. However, if you tried to put the word 'in' with 'doubtable', this would not be grammatically correct.

Q2. On

EXPLANATION = if you added the word 'on' to the following words, you would make: oncoming, ongoing, onshore and online.

Q3. C = low

EXPLANATION = low is the odd one out because it is pronounced differently from the other three words.

Q4. A = obtuse

EXPLANATION = 'resourceful', 'astute' and 'adept' are all words that can be associated with the word 'smart'. 'Obtuse' is a word that can be defined as "annoyingly insensitive or slow to understand". Therefore it doesn't carry the same meaning as the other three words.

Q5. B = reference

EXPLANATION = if you were to put the word 'in' with the words 'decisive', 'destructible' and 'convenience', you would get: indecisive, indestructible and inconvenience. However, if you were to put the word 'in' with the word 'reference', this would be grammatically incorrect. This would need to be two separate words, i.e. in reference to, so this is the word that cannot be linked with the word outside the bracket.

Q6. A = run

EXPLANATION = if you were to put 'can' with the words 'apé', 'did' and 'cellation', you would get the following words; canapé, candid and cancellation. However, if you put the word 'can' with 'run', this is not grammatically correct.

Q7. D = sit

EXPLANATION = the word 'sit' is the odd one out because all of the other words refer to a type of exercise.

Q8. A = sort

EXPLANATION = 'sort' can mean a 'type of' or 'variety' of something i.e. a type of tree. Or it can mean to sort things, 'to arrange' and 'organise'.

Q9. B = 'b'

EXPLANATION = if you removed the 'b' from the word 'tribal' you would get 'trial'. If you added it to the second word you would get 'robbed'.

Q10. Match

EXPLANATION = matchmaking, matchwood, matchstick and matchbox.

Q11. D = Strong

EXPLANATION = in order to find the best word to fill in the gap, you need to understand the structure of the sentence. In this sentence, the best word that would fit is 'strong'. We know that the news reporter has very little time to conduct with his interview, so his questions cannot be lengthy. It also makes no sense for his questions to be cruel, or boring. Therefore, in order to gain as much information in as little time as possible, his questions will have to be 'strong.'

Q12. B = December

EXPLANATION = December is the odd one out because all of the other months occur consecutively to each other, May-June-July. December, on the other hand, is several months apart.

Q13. D = feasible

EXPLANATION = the correct word that would fit in the structure of the sentence is 'feasible'. 'Feasable' and 'feasability' are not words; they are just an incorrect spelling of feasible and feasibility.

Q14. C = cow

EXPLANATION = the words beef, mutton, pork and ham are all words used to describe types of meat. Cow is the animal from which we get beef/a type of meat, and therefore is the odd one out.

Q15. B = affraid

EXPLANATION = 'affraid' is the odd one out because all of the other words are spelt correctly, whereas 'affraid' should be spelt 'afraid'.

Q16. D = ivory

EXPLANATION = 'ivory' is the odd one out because all of the other words refer to a type of metal, whereas ivory is not a type of metal, it is a creamy-white substance composing the main part of the tusks of an elephant, walrus etc.

Q17. E - The bouncer was pushed by a man who then fell to the floor.

EXPLANATION = all of the other sentences refer to the bouncer pushing a man to the floor. However the sentence 'the bouncer was pushed by a man who then fell to the floor' has a different meaning to all of the other sentences.

Q18. In

EXPLANATION = you can use the word 'in' to make the following new words: inadequate, intake, invisible and intuition.

Q19. D = cendible

EXPLANATION = if you were to put 'dis' with 'affirm', 'abuse', and 'accorded', you would get: disaffirm, disabuse and disaccorded. However, if you tried to put 'dis' with 'cendible', this would not be grammatically correct.

Q20. C = truments

EXPLANATION = if you were to put 'int' with the words 'egumentary', 'ellect' and 'elligble', you would get: integumentary, intellect, and intelligible. However, if you tried to put 'int' with 'truments', this would not be grammatically correct. You would need to add 'ins' to 'truments' to get 'instruments'.

Q21. Inter

EXPLANATION = the five letter word 'inter' can be added to all of the words to create the following new words: intertitle, interplay, interview and interpose.

Q22. Dead

EXPLANATION = the four letter word 'dead' can be added to all of the words to create the following new words: deadweight, deadwood, deadbolt and deadlock.

Q23. Over

EXPLANATION = the four letter word 'over' can be added to all of the words to create the following new words: overreact, overloaded, overcast and overdrive.

Q24. D = race

EXPLANATION = 'race' can mean either a 'competition/running', or can refer to a person's 'origin'.

Q25. A = 31st June 1999

EXPLANATION = the 31st June 1999 is the odd one out because this date does not exist. There is not 31 days in the month of June.

Q26. A = dragon

EXPLANATION = dragon is the odd one out because all of the other animals are real, whereas a dragon is a mythological creature.

Q27. C = Tokyo

EXPLANATION = Tokyo is the odd one out because all of the other words are countries, whereas Tokyo is a city.

Q28. D = anvil

EXPLANATION = Anvil is the odd one out because all of the other words are words that you would normally associate with boating, or ships.

Q29. C = bark

EXPLANATION = 'bark' can mean 'part of a tree', or the bark 'woof' sound that a dog makes.

Q30. C = reat

EXPLANATION = if you put the word 'rat' with the words 'able', 'fishes' and 'line', you would get the following: rateable, ratfishes and ratline. However, if you tried to put 'rat' with 'reat', this would be grammatically incorrect. You could put 'ret' with 'reat' to give you the new word 'retreat', but as it stands the word 'ratreat' does not work.

ROYAL NAVY RECRUITING TEST – NUMERICAL

As part of your Royal Navy Recruiting test, you will be required to take a Numerical Reasoning test; one of four sub-sections of your assessment.

The Numerical Reasoning part of your Royal Navy Recruiting test is to assess a candidate's ability to make accurate calculations using basic mathematical formulas including:

- Addition
- Subtraction
- Multiplication
- Division
- Percentage, Decimals and Fractions
- Algebra
- Area and Perimeter
- Significant Figures

We suggest that you practice as many different types of mathematical questions as you can prior to your assessment. The following Numerical tests will include all the typical question types that more often than not, crop up in the Royal Navy Recruiting test.

On the day of your RN assessment, **you will have 16 minutes in which to answer the 30 questions** relating to Numerical Reasoning. In your real test, please note that you will be given a separate sheet of paper in which you indicate your answers, however for the purpose of this book, we would like you to indicate your answer underneath the question by highlighting or writing your answer.

In order to gain some understanding of the types of questions you will face during this sub-test, and how you go about answering them, check out the following pages of example questions. These examples provide clear and detailed descriptions of how to answer the question correctly, what to expect, what to look out for, and useful tips regarding each question type.

Good luck.

EXAMPLES OF
NUMERICAL
REASONING

Areas and Perimeters

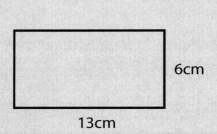

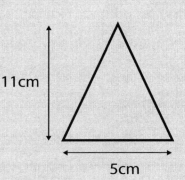

Area of squares/ rectangles

Base x height

- 13 x 6 = 78 cm²

Area of triangles

½ base x height

- 11 x 5 ÷ 2 = 27.5

Perimeter

Add all the sizes of each side.

- 6 + 6 + 13 + 13 = 38

Angles

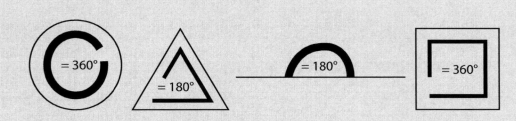

Fractions / Decimals / Percentages

$$\frac{1}{10} = 0.1 = 10\%$$

How to work out fractions into decimals into percentages:

- To convert 0.1 into a percent, you would move the decimal point two places to the right, so it becomes 10%.

- To convert 1/10 into a decimal, you would divide both numbers. For example, $1 \div 10 = 0.1$.

- To convert 10% into a decimal, you move the decimal point two places to the left. For example, to convert 10% into a decimal, the decimal point moves two spaces to the left to become 0.1.

Fractions

$$\text{What is } \frac{3}{7} \text{ of 700?}$$

How to work it out:

- $700 \div 7 \times 3 = 300$

Adding Fractions

$$\frac{5}{7} + \frac{3}{5}$$

$$\frac{5}{7} \times \frac{3}{5} = \frac{25 + 21}{35} = \frac{46}{35} = 1\frac{46}{35}$$

Crossbow Method:

- The CROSS looks like a multiplication sign and it tells you which numbers to multiply together.

- One arm is saying 'multiply the 5 by the 5', and the other arm is saying 'multiply the 7 by the 3'.

- The BOW says 'multiply the 2 numbers I am pointing at'. That is 7 times 5.

- The answer is 35 and it goes underneath the line in the answer.

Subtracting Fractions

$$\frac{4}{7} - \frac{2}{5}$$

$$\frac{4}{7} \times \frac{2}{5} = \frac{20 - 14}{35} = \frac{6}{35}$$

- To subtract fractions, the method is exactly the same. The only difference is, you minus the two numbers forming the top of the fraction, as opposed to adding them.

Multiplying Fractions

$$\frac{2}{3} \times \frac{4}{7}$$

$$\frac{2}{3} \times \frac{4}{7} = \frac{8}{21}$$

Arrow Method:

- Multiplying fractions is easy. Draw two arrows through the two top numbers of the fraction, and then draw a line through the two bottom numbers (as shown above) and then multiply – simple!

- Sometimes the fraction can be simplified, but in the above example, the answer is already in its simplest form.

Dividing Fractions

$$\frac{3}{7} \div \frac{1}{3}$$

$$\frac{3}{7} \times \frac{3}{1} = \frac{3}{7} \times \frac{3}{1} = \frac{9}{7} = 1\frac{2}{7}$$

- Most people think that dividing fractions is difficult. But, it's not! Actually, it's relatively simple if you have mastered multiplying fractions.

- Mathematicians realised that if you turned the second fraction upside down (like in the above example), and then change the 'divide' sum to a 'multiply', you will get the correct answer – every time!

Ratios

Ben has some sweets. He is going to share them with his two friends. Ben has 24 sweets and is going to share them in the ratio of 4 : 2 : 3.

How many sweets does each person get?

- Add up the ratios = 4 + 2 + 2 = 8
- 24 ÷ 8 = 3.
- So, 3 × 4 = 12.
- 3 × 2 = 6.
- 3 × 2 = 6.

So one person will have 12 sweets and the two other people will get 6 sweets.

Significant Figures / Decimal Places

Rounding up to Significant Figures:

What is 7.9942 to two significant figures?

- For the above example, you have to round up.
- The two significant figures are 7 and 9. The digit after the 9 is 9 again, so we have to round up to 8.00.

Rounding up to decimal places:

This is simple, if the question asks you to round up to three decimal places, you count the numbers of decimal places (3) backwards (i.e. to the left), and then use the next number to either round up or round down.

What is 2.6249 to three decimal places?

- The answer would be 2.625
- You find the number that is 3 decimal places, and then use the next number to decide whether to round up or round down.

NUMERICAL REASONING - *TEST 1*

(You have 16 minutes in which to complete the 30 questions).

Question 1

If the perimeter of a square is 40cm, then the area of the square, in square centimetres, is…

A	B	C	D	E
50	80	100	110	200

Question 2

5879 − 4528 =

A	B	C	D	E
1451	1221	1351	1521	1531

Question 3

What is 5/8 as a percentage?

A	B	C	D
60.5%	62.5%	68.5%	63.8%

Question 4

What is 7/11 as a decimal? Rounded up to two decimal places.

A	B	C	D
0.12	0.73	0.64	0.61

Question 5

A square has an area of 121cm². What is the perimeter of the rectangle?

A	B	C	D	E
44 inches	44 cm	242 cm	242 inches	110 cm

Question 6

What is 47.889097 to three significant figures?

Answer

Question 7

What is 69.969097 to three significant figures?

Answer

Question 8

If you count from 1-100, how many numbers that contain the number '3' will you encounter?

A	B	C	D	E
20	19	11	12	21

Question 9

During the Royal Navy Recruiting test, a candidate achieves 40%. If the maximum possible score was 90, what score did the candidate achieve?

A	B	C	D	E
34	35	36	44	45

Question 10

What is 2 ¼ + 3 ½? Write your answer as a mixed fraction and in its simplest form.

Answer

Question 11

Calculate 44 x 22.

A	B	C	D	E
886	968	986	689	896

Question 12

A die is thrown 420 times and the number 6 is obtained 63 times; express the frequency of obtaining the number 6 as a percentage.

A	B	C	D	E
13%	14%	15%	16%	17%

Question 13

Calculate 21.1 x 3

A	B	C	D	E
633	62.3	63.3	623	66.6

Question 14

What is the percentage decrease between 45 and 27?

A	B	C	D	E
25%	18%	30%	40%	56%

Question 15

What is 24% of 80 and then minus 6?

A	B	C	D	E
11.2	9.2	17.2	13.2	14

Question 16

If r = 41 and s = 966, then s − r =

A	B	C	D	E
295	95	925	935	915

Question 17

The clock below reads 3pm. How many degrees will the small (hour) hand have turned when the time reaches 9pm?

A	B	C	D	E
180°	90°	360°	60°	30°

Question 18

What is 1300 x 0.6?

A	B	C	D	E
7,800	78	990	780	870

Question 19

Mia has £4.50. Ellie has £6.50.

What is the ratio of Mia's money to Ellie's money, in its simplest form?

A	B	C	D	E
4 : 6	3 : 5	7 : 11	7 : 13	9 : 13

Question 20

The clock below reads 3am. How many degrees will the large (hour) hand have turned when the time reaches 3pm?

A	B	C	D	E
4320°	360°	180°	90°	270°

Question 21

The clock below reads 3pm. How many degrees will the large (minute) hand have turned when the time reaches 4:45pm?

A	B	C	D	E
105°	270°	320°	405°	630°

Question 22

A student scored 51/60 in their test. What is their test score as a percent?

A	B	C	D
65%	85%	90%	75%

Question 23

A triangle has the height of 14cm and the length of 18cm. What is the area of the triangle?

A	B	C	D
113	134	126	129

Question 24

What is 770 x 0.1?

A	B	C	D
77	7,700	770	170

Question 25

A student has been prescribed medication by her doctor. She is prescribed a 10.5 fluid ounce bottle of medication with the instructions to take 0.25 fluid ounces twice a day. How many days/weeks does she have to take the medication for?

A	B	C	D
7 days	3 days	3 weeks	2 weeks

Question 26

What is 5/8 x 3/5? In its simplest form.

A	B	C	D
2/3	6/7	5/8	3/8

Question 27

What is 5,628 rounded to the nearest thousand?

A	B	C	D
5,000	5,600	6,000	5,500

Question 28

What is the number 44.978832 correct to three decimal places?

A	B	C	D	E
44.9	44.978	44.979	45.0	44.98

Question 29

A teacher needs to mark 42 test papers. Each test takes approximately 9 minutes to mark. She also spends 3 minutes checking over each report. How long in hours and minutes will it take for the teacher to finish marking the test papers?

A	B	C	D	E
8 hours and 16 minutes	7 hours and 45 minutes	8 hours and 24 minutes	7 hours and 54 minutes	9 hours

Question 30

What is the percentage profit or loss if the buying price is £290 and the selling price is £237.80?

A	B	C	D
18% profit	24% profit	18% loss	24% loss

ANSWERS TO NUMERICAL REASONING – SECTION 1

Q1. C = 100

EXPLANATION = if the perimeter of a square is 40cm, that means each side of the square needs to be 10cm (10 + 10 + 10 + 10 = 40). So, to work out the area, you would multiply the height of the square by the length of the square (10 x 10 = 100). So, the correct answer is 100.

Q2. C = 1351

EXPLANATION = 5879 – 4528 = 1351.

Q3. B = 62.5%

EXPLANATION = 5⁄8 of 100 = 5 ÷ 8 = 0.625. As a percentage = 0.625 x 100 = 62.5%.

Q4. C = 0.64

EXPLANATION = 7⁄11 of 100% = 7 ÷ 11 = 0.636. To two decimal places = 0.64.

Q5. B = 44 cm

EXPLANATION = a square has an area of 121 cm². So, in order to work out the perimeter of the square you need to find the square root of 121. So, this would be 11 (11 x 11 = 121). So, the perimeter of the square will be: 11 + 11 + 11 + 11 = 44 cm.

Q6. 47.9

EXPLANATION = 47.889097, to three significant figures, is 47.9

Q7. 70.0

EXPLANATION = 69.969097, to three significant figures, is 70.0.

Q8. A = 20

EXPLANATION = if you counted all the numbers from 1 to 100, the number of '3's' that would be seen is 20. (3, 13, 23, 30, 31, 32, 33, 34, 35, 36, 37, 38, 39, 43, 53, 63, 73, 83, 93).

Q9. C = 36

EXPLANATON = for this question, you need to work out 40% of 90. So, 90 ÷ 100 x 40 = 36. So, 40% of 90 is 36.

Q10. 5 3/4

EXPLANATION = 2 ¼ is equivalent to 9/4.

3 ½ is equivalent to 7/2.

$$\frac{9}{4} \times \frac{7}{2} = \frac{(9 \times 2) + (4 \times 7)}{8} = \frac{46}{8} = \frac{23}{4} = 5\frac{3}{4}$$

Q11. B = 968

EXPLANATION = 44 x 20 = 880.

44 x 2 = 88.

So, 88 + 880 = 968.

Q12. C = 15%

EXPLANATION = 63/420 = 3/20 = 100 ÷ 20 x 3 = 15%.

Q13. C = 63.3

EXPLANATION = in order to work out these types of questions, it is best to take out the decimal point, do the calculation, and then add in the decimal point at the end.

So, 211 x 3 = 633. Remember, the decimal point has one number after it, and so the answer will need one number after the decimal point. Move the decimal point one place to the left of 633, which will give you 63.3, and this is your answer.

Q14. D = 40%

EXPLANATION = in order to work out the percentage decrease you need to find the difference between the two numbers. So, 45 – 27 = 18. So, there is a difference of 18. Now you need to do the following 18 ÷ 45 x 100 = 40%.

Q15. D = 13.2

EXPLANATION = 80 ÷ 100 x 24 = 19.2. 19.2 – 6 = 13.2.

Q16. C = 925

EXPLANATION = if s = 966, and you need to minus r = 41, 966 – 41 = 925.

Q17. A = 180°

EXPLANATION = in order for the small hour hand to go from 3 to 9 on the clock, it must rotate 180°. You know this because 3 and 9 are opposite each other on the clock and therefore form a straight line. A straight line makes an angle of 180°.

Q18. D = 780

EXPLANATION = in order to work out these types of questions, it is best to take out the decimal point, do the calculation, and then add in the decimal point at the end.

So, 1,300 x 06 (which is just 6) = 7,800. Remember, the decimal point has one number after it, and so the answer will need on number after the number after the decimal point. Move the decimal point one place to the left of 7,800, which will give you 780.0 (or just 780), and this is your answer.

Q19. E = 9 : 13

EXPLANATION: Both amounts are in pounds. We have to convert both amounts into pence. £4.50 = 450p. £6.50 = 650p. Now the ratio is 450 : 650. Both sides are divisible by 50. Dividing both sides by 50 gives 9 : 13. So the ratio is 9 : 13.

Q20. A = 4320°

EXPLANATION = from 3am to 3pm that's 12 hours. Therefore the large hand of the clock needs to move 12 whole hours to reach 3pm. So, 12 x 360 (a circle has a 360° rotation) = 4320°.

Q21. E = 630°

EXPLANATION = to get from 3pm to 4.45 pm, that is one hour and 45 minutes, So, the large hand will have to rotate one whole hour (one whole circle = 360°). To work out how many degrees there is from the large hand starting on the 12 to the 9 (equivalent to 45 minutes), you need to divide 360 by 12 (number of hours on the clock) and then multiply it by 9 (9 is 45 minutes, which is what you need to work out). So, 360 ÷ 12 = 30 x 9 = 270. So, 360 + 270 = 630° rotation is needed to get from 3pm to 4.45pm.

Q22. B = 85%

EXPLANATION = to work out the percentage score for a student who scored 51 out of 60, you will need to do the following: 51 ÷ 60 = 0.85 (this gives you the decimal). In order to work out the percentage, you need to multiply the decimal by 100 = 0.85 x 100 = 85%.

Q23. C = 126

EXPLANATION = to work out the area of a triangle, you need to remember the following formula: base x height ÷ 2. So, 14 x 18 = 252 ÷ 2 = 126.

Q24. A = 77

EXPLANATION = in order to work out these types of questions, it is best to take out the decimal point, do the calculation, and then add in the decimal point at the end.

So, 770 x 0.1 (which is just 1) = 770. Remember, the decimal point has one number after it, and so the answer will need on number after the number after the decimal point. Move the decimal point one place to the left of 770, which will give you 77.0 (or just 77), and this is your answer.

Q25. C = 3 weeks

EXPLANATION = she is prescribed a 10.5 fluid ounce bottle of medication with the instructions to take 0.25 fluid ounces twice a day. So, she will be taking 0.50 fluid ounces a day (she has to take it twice daily). So, you need to work out how long the 10.5 fluid ounce bottle will last her, if she is taking 0.50 fluid ounces a day.

So, 10.5 ÷ 0.50. (It is best to take out the decimal point, do the calculation, and then add in the decimal point at the end). 105 ÷ 50 = 2.1. Now move the decimal point, one space to the right = 21 days / 3 weeks.

Q26. D = 3/8

EXPLANATION = to work out how you multiply fractions, use the formula as shown below:

$$\frac{5}{8} \times \frac{3}{5} = \frac{5 \times 3}{8 \times 5} = \frac{15}{40} = \frac{3}{8}$$

Q27. C = 6,000

EXPLANATION = to work out how to round numbers up or down, you need to work out what part of the number you need to focus on. The question is asking you to round up to the nearest thousand, so the important part to look at in the question is the (5) thousand. In this instance, 5600 is closer to 6000 than it is 5000. Therefore it should be rounded up to 6000.

Q28. C = 44.979

EXPLANATION = the third number after the decimal point is 8. So, in order to work out the correct number to three decimal points, you need to work out whether this number is being rounded up or rounded down. The number after the 8 is 9, and numbers higher than 5 are rounded up, and therefore the correct number would be 44.979.

Q29. C = 8 hours and 24 minutes

EXPLANATION = the teacher spends 9 minutes marking and 3 minutes checking each report. That is 12 minutes in total for each paper. She has 42 papers to mark. So 42 x 12 = 504 minutes. The question asks you to convert this into hours and minutes, and so this is equivalent to 8 hours and 24 minutes.

Q30. C = 18% loss

EXPLANATION = 290 − 237.80 = 52.20 ÷ 290 x 100 = 18% loss.

NUMERICAL REASONING - TEST 2

(You have 16 minutes in which to complete the 30 questions).

Question 1

Alison has been keeping a record of how much she has been withdrawing from the cash point machine. Over the last 8 weeks she has withdrawn the following amounts:

£10   £25   £60   £60   £20   £10   £90   £100

What percentage of her withdrawals are under £60?

A	B	C	D	E
40%	50%	60%	70%	65%

Question 2

Calculate 3/8 ÷ 3/4.

A	B	C	D	E
1/2	2/25	3/4	1/8	2/32

Question 3

42 out of 120 hospital patients have leg injuries. What percentage of patients have leg injuries?

A	B	C	D	E
25%	54%	46%	50%	35%

Question 4

The clock below reads 3pm. How many degrees will the large (minute) hand have turned when the time reaches 4pm?

A	B	C	D	E
360°	12°	180°	460°	45°

Question 5

The clock below reads 3pm. How many degrees will the small (hour) hand have turned when the time reaches 8pm?

A	B	C	D	E
1440°	150°	50°	270°	45°

Question 6

Fill in the question mark.

2 x 3.8 ? 7.3

A	B	C	D
>	=	<	+

Question 7

Put these decimals in order from smallest to biggest.

2.22   22.2   0.2   2.02

A	B	C	D
2.02 0.2 22.2 2.22	2.22 0.2 22.2 2.02	0.2 2.02 2.22 22.2	22.2 2.22 2.02 0.2

Question 8

What is 4/9 as a percentage?

A	B	C	D
44.4%	27.4%	48.9%	54.5%

Question 9

Susan draws 4 squares and 3 triangles. How many degrees are there altogether?

A	B	C	D
980°	880°	1980°	1890°

Question 10

Calculate 7/9 - 2/3. In its simplest form.

A	B	C	D
3/27	1/9	4/9	2/3

Question 11

Convert 0.75 to a fraction.

A	B	C	D
1/75	3/4	7/5	2/5

Question 12

One side of a rectangle is 30 cm. If the area of the rectangle is 570 cm², what is the length of the other side?

A	B	C	D	E
15cm	17cm	6cm	7cm	19cm

Question 13

Melissa bought a new necklace. 70% of the 20 beads on her necklace were pink. How many pink beads are there on Melissa's necklace?

A	B	C	D
11	13	14	17

Question 14

What is the lowest common multiple of 8 and 2?

A	B	C	D
8	16	2	1

Question 15

What is 2/9 x 9? Simplify your answer and write it as a proper fraction or as a whole or mixed number.

A	B	C	D
9/18	2 1/9	2	9/17

Question 16

What is 888 ÷ 8?

A	B	C	D	E
422	444	222	111	224

Question 17

Mike draws two squares, six triangles and a circle. How many degrees are there altogether?

A	B	C	D
2160°	2260°	2240°	1640°

Question 18

The clock below reads 3pm. How many degrees will the small (hour) hand have turned when the time reaches 11pm?

A	B	C	D	E
45°	8°	240°	80°	270°

Question 19

How many bricks, each measuring 22 cm x 11cm x 8 cm, will be needed to build a wall of 8m x 6m x 25 cm?

A	B	C	D
6135	6192	6198	9817

Question 20

In July, Ryan worked a total of 40 hours, in August he worked 46.5 hours. By what percentage did Ryan's working hours increase in August?

A	B	C	D
16.25%	165%	1.625%	25%

Question 21

What is 0.9 as a percentage?

A	B	C	D
0.009%	0.9%	9%	90%

Question 22

Work out 23.7 − 2.5 × 8.

A	B	C	D
169.6	134.6	169.9	166.9

Question 23

What is the highest common factor of 12 and 20?

A	B	C	D
4	8	12	2

Question 24

What is 6/8 ÷ 2/3? Use mixed fractions to simplify your answer.

A	B	C	D
5/8	1/8	2 1/8	1 1/8

Question 25

Multiply 0.04 by 1.1.

A	B	C	D
0.011	0.1414	0.044	0.144

Question 26

Add 7/9 of 189 to 5/8 of 128.

A	B	C	D
207	217	227	277

Question 27

There were 17 million families in the UK in 2006.

The mean number of children per family was 1.8.

How many children were there in the UK?

A	B	C	D
30.6 million	306 million	3.6 million	36 million

Question 28

John wants to lose 16 kilograms in weight. After 4 months he has lost ¾ of this amount. How much has John lost?

A	B	C	D	E
5 kg	4 kg	7 kg	12 kg	8 kg

Question 29

The population of the world in 1960 was 3040 million. In 1975, it was 4090 million. It is considered that the population grows by a constant percentage each year.

What constant annual percentage growth rate from 1960 to 1975 would result in the population increasing from 3040 million to 4090 million?

A	B	C	D
5 %	8 %	2 %	3 %

Question 30

Work out the following sum:

(41 + 21) – 3 = ? + 45

A	B	C	D	E
11	12	13	14	15

ANSWERS TO NUMERICAL REASONING – SECTION 2

Q1. B = 50%

EXPLANATION = Alison went to the cash machine 8 times. Out of those 8 times, she withdrew under £60, four times. So this can be put in the fraction of 4/8, which is equivalent to 1/2, which as a percentage = 50%.

Q2. A = ½

EXPLANATION = in order to work out how to divide fractions, you use the same method as if you were multiplying, the only difference is, you need to turn the last fraction upside down, and then multiply them together. Use the following method:

$$\frac{3}{8} \div \frac{3}{4} = \frac{3}{8} \times \frac{4}{3} = \frac{3 \times 4}{8 \times 3} = \frac{12}{24} = \frac{6}{12} = \frac{3}{6} = \frac{1}{2}$$

Q3. E = 35%

EXPLANATION = 42 ÷ 120 x 100 = 35%.

Q4. A = 360°

EXPLANATION = in order to work out how many degrees the large hand of the clock rotates from 3pm to 4pm, you need to work out the difference in time. So, the difference in time is 1 hour. That means the large hand needs to rotate a whole turn (one hour requires a whole rotation of the large hand), and therefore the large hand must rotate 360° degrees.

Q5. B = 150°

EXPLANATION = in order to work out how many degrees the small hand of the clock rotates from 3pm until 8pm, you need to work out the difference in time. From 3pm to 8pm is 5 hours difference. Using the 3 and the 9 as a 180° line, you can work out what degree the small hand will have moved So, 180 ÷ 6 (numbers under the line) = 30. So, 30 x 5 (from 8 - 3 = 5) = 150°.

Q6. A = '>'

EXPLANATION = 2 x 3.8 = 7.6. Therefore this is higher than 7.3. This would be displayed with a '>' sign, which indicates the bigger number/points towards the smaller number.

Q7. C = 0.2   2.02   2.22   22.2

EXPLANATION = from smallest to biggest = 0.2, 2.02, 2.22 and 22.2. Pay careful attention to where the decimal point is placed.

Q8. A = 44.4%

EXPLANATION = 4/9 as a percentage = 4 ÷ 9 = 0.4444. To turn this decimal in to a percentage = 0.4444 x 100 = 44.4%

Q9. C = 1980°

EXPLANATION = 4 squares = 360 x 4 = 1440. 3 triangles = 180 x 3 = 540. So, 1440 + 540 = 1980°.

Q10. B = 1 /9

EXPLANATION = in order to work out how to subtract fractions, you can use the following method:

$$\frac{7}{9} \times \frac{2}{3} = \frac{(7 \times 3) + (9 \times 2)}{27} = \frac{3}{27} = \frac{1}{9}$$

Although answer A is technically correct, the question specifically asks for the answer in its simplest form, so make sure you read the question carefully.

Q11. B = 3/4

EXPLANATION = to convert 0.75 into a fraction, you need to know the correct method. 0.75 as a percentage = 0.75 x 100 = 75%. 0.75 is equivalent to 75 out of 100 (75/100), which can be simplified to 3/4.

Q12. E = 19cm

EXPLANATION = if one side of a rectangle is 30cm, and the area of the rectangle is 570cm², to work out the other length of the rectangle: 570 ÷ 30 = 19cm. So, 19 x 30 (length x height = area) = 570cm². So, the correct answer is 19cm.

Q13. C = 14

EXPLANATION = 20 ÷ 100 x 70 = 14.

Q14. A = 8

EXPLANATION = multiples of 8 are 8, 16, 24, 32, 40. The multiples of 2 are 2, 4, 6, 8, 10. Therefore the lowest multiple for 8 and 2 is 8.

Q15. C = 2

EXPLANATION = first of all you need to change 9 to a fraction (9/1). So 2/9 x 9/1 = 2 x 9, over 9 x 1 = 18/9 = 2.

Q16. D = 111

EXPLANATION = 888 ÷ 8 = 111.

Q17. A = 2160°

EXPLANATION = two squares = 360 x 2 = 720. Six triangles = 180 x 6 = 1080. One circle = 360. So, 720 + 1080 + 360 = 2160.

Q18. C = 240°

EXPLANATION = in order to work out how many degrees the small hand will have turned from 3pm to 11pm, you need to work out the difference in time, and that difference is 8 hours. For the small hand to reach 11pm, it will rotate 8 turns out of the possible 12 hours. So, 360 ÷ 12 (number of hours on the clock) x 8 (number of times it needs to rotate) = 240°.

Q19. C = 6198

EXPLANATION = Number of bricks = Volume of the wall ÷ volume of 1 brick = 800 x 600 x 25 = 12,000,000.

Volume of 1 brick = 22 x 11 x 8 = 1936. So, 12,000,000 ÷ 1936 = 6198.

Q20. A = 16.25%

EXPLANATION = To tackle this problem, we need to calculate the difference in hours between the new and old numbers. 46.5 - 40 hours = 6.5 hours. We can see that Ryan worked 6.5 hours more in August than he did in July – this is his increase.

To work out the increase as a percentage it is now necessary to divide the increase by the original (January) number: 6.5 ÷ 40 = 0.1625

Finally, to get the percentage we multiply the answer by 100. This simply means moving the decimal place two columns to the right. 0.1625 × 100 = 16.25. Ryan therefore worked 16.25% more hours in August than he did in July.

Q21. D = 90%

EXPLANATION = 0.9 x 100 = 90%.

Q22. A = 169.6

EXPLANATION = 23.7 – 2.5 = 21.2 x 8 = 169.6.

Q23. A = 4

EXPLANATION = the factors of 12 are: 1, 2, 3, 4, 6 and 12. The factors of 20 are: 1, 2, 4, 5 and 20. So the highest common factor for 12 and 20 is 4.

Q24. D = 1 1/8

EXPLANATION = an easy way to remember how to divide fractions is to turn the last fraction upside down, and then multiply.

So, 2/3 becomes 3/2. So, 6 x 3 = 18 and 8 x 2 = 16. This gives you the fraction: 18/16 = 9/8 = 1 1/8.

Q25. C = 0.044

EXPLANATION = in order to work out how to multiply decimals, multiply the numbers normally, ignoring the decimal points. Then put the decimal points back into the answer. Remember, it will have as many decimal places as the two original numbers combined. So, 4 x 11 = 33.

To get 4 from 0.04, it has 2 decimal places. To get 11 from 1.1, it has 1 decimal place. Therefore your answer needs to contain 3 numbers after the decimal point = 0.044.

Q26. C = 227

EXPLANATION = 189 ÷ 9 x 7 = 147.

128 ÷ 8 x 5 = 80.

So, 80 + 147 = 227.

Q27. A = 30.6 million

EXPLANATION = 17,000,000 (number of families in the UK) x 1.8 (mean number of children per family) = 30,600,000 = 30.6 million.

Q28. D = 12 kg

EXPLANATION = John wants to lose 16 kg. He has lost 3/4 of this so far. So, to work out how many kilograms he has lost: 16 ÷ 4 x 3 = 12 kg.

Q29. C = 2 per cent

EXPLANATION = 4090 − 3040 = 1050.

So, 1050 ÷ 4090 x 100 = 25.67.

25.67 ÷ 15 (number of years between 1960 and 1975) = 1.71. Round up to nearest whole number = 2%.

Q30. D = 14

EXPLANATION = (41 + 21) = 62 − 3 = 59. So, 59 − 45 = 14. So, 14 is the missing number in the sum.

ROYAL NAVY RECRUITING TEST – MECHANICAL COMPREHENSION

As part of your Royal Navy Recruiting test, you will be required to take a Mechanical Comprehension test; one of four sub-sections of your assessment.

The Mechanical Comprehension part of your Royal Navy Recruiting test is to assess your mechanical and technical understanding. These types of questions often relate to:

- Gears and Pulleys
- Springs
- Weights
- Levers
- Rotating objects

Mechanical Comprehension tests are an assessment that measures an individual's ability to understand mechanical concepts. The tests are usually multiple-choice and present simple encountered mechanisms and technical situations. The majority of Mechanical Comprehension tests require a working knowledge of basic mechanical operations and the application of physical laws.

On the day of your RN assessment, **you will have 10 minutes in which to answer the 30 questions** relating to Mechanical Comprehension. In your real test, please note that you will be given a separate sheet of paper in which you indicate your answers, however for the purpose of this book, we would like you to indicate your answer underneath the question by highlighting or writing your answer.

In order to gain some understanding of the types of questions you will face during this sub-test, and how you go about answering them, check out the following pages of example questions. These examples provide clear and detailed descriptions of how to answer the question correctly, what to expect, what to look out for, and useful tips regarding each question type.

Good luck.

EXAMPLES OF
MECHANICAL
COMPREHENSION

Levers and Force

A lever consists of a bar which is balanced on a fixed point, known as the fulcrum.

If you needed to lift the weight, you need to work out how to calculate the force needed.

Formula:

Force needed = (weight x distance from fulcrum to weight) ÷ distance from fulcrum point where force is being applied.

Example:

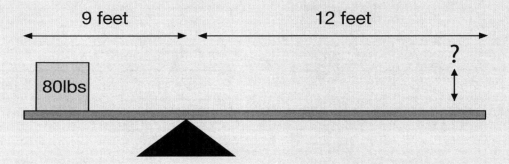

- F = (weight x distance from fulcrum to weight) ÷ distance from fulcrum to point where force is being applied.
- F = (80 x 9) ÷ 12
- F = 720 ÷ 12
- F = 60 lbs

Answer:

60 lbs

Pulleys

Single and Double Pulleys

If the pulley is fixed, then the force required is equal to the weight. A simple way to work out how to calculate the force that is required, is to divide the weight by the number of sections of rope supporting it.

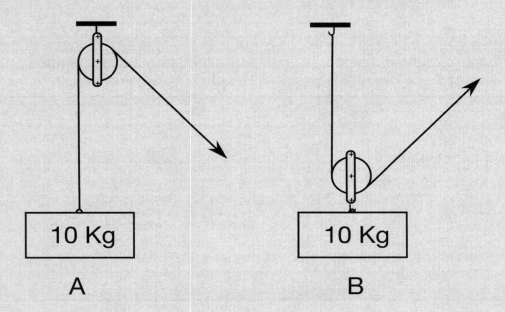

Diagram A = there is only one section of rope supporting the weight, therefore this can be worked out by = 10 ÷ 1 = 10.

Diagram B = there are two ropes supporting the weight, therefore this can be worked out by: 10 (weight) ÷ 2 (number of ropes supporting the weight) = 5.

Gears

If gears are connected by a chain or belt, then the gears will all move in the same direction.

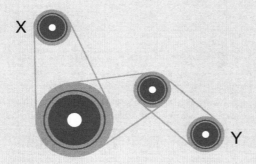

If the gears are touching, then adjacent gears move in the opposite direction. In the example below, X and Y will move in opposite directions.

Springs

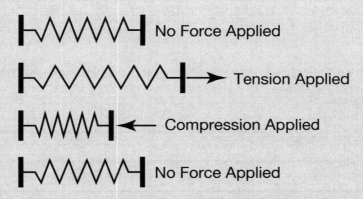

No Force Applied

Tension Applied

Compression Applied

No Force Applied

Spring Under Tension & Compression

When springs are arranged in a series, each spring can be the subject of the force applied. If the springs are arranged in a parallel line, the force is divided equally between them.

Circuits

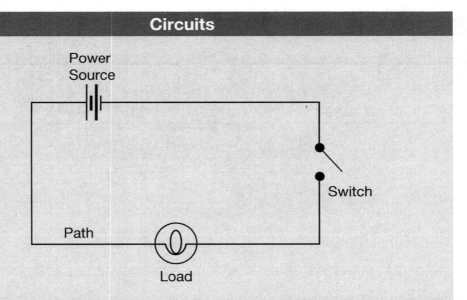

Questions regarding circuits usually follow a similar circuit, which will include: a power source, switches, bulbs and a path of wiring.

MECHANICAL COMPREHENSION - *TEST 1*

(You have 10 minutes in which to complete the 30 questions).

Question 1

Which weight requires the most force to lift it?

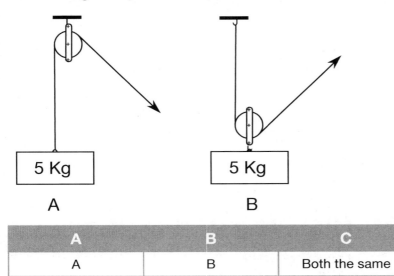

A	B	C
A	B	Both the same

Question 2

How much weight is required to balance point X?

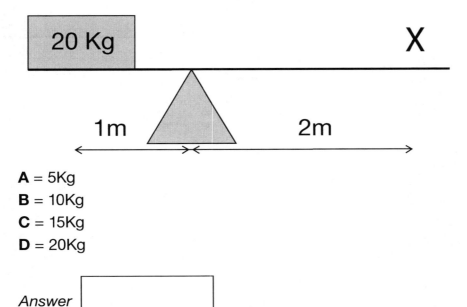

A = 5Kg
B = 10Kg
C = 15Kg
D = 20Kg

Answer

Question 3

If cog C turns anti-clockwise at a speed of 10rpm, which way and at what speed will cog B turn?

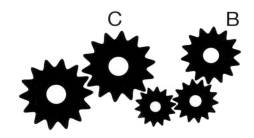

A	B	C	D
10rpm / anti-clockwise	10rpm / clockwise	20 rpm / anti-clockwise	20 rpm / clockwise

Question 4

Which tool would you use to claw nails from wood?

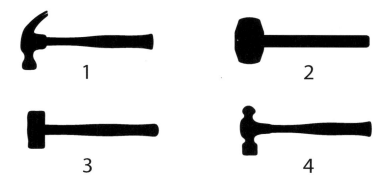

A	B	C	D
1	2	3	4

Question 5

If bulb 2 is removed which bulbs will illuminate?

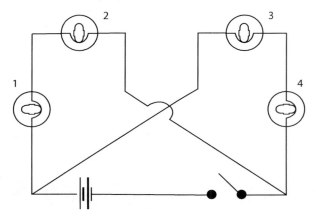

A	B	C	D
1	3	4	None

Question 6

When the switch is closed, how many bulbs will illuminate when bulb 3 is removed?

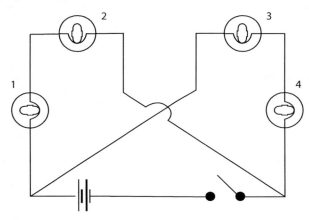

A	B	C	D
None	One	Two	Three

Question 7

If cog B turns anti-clockwise which way will cog A turn?

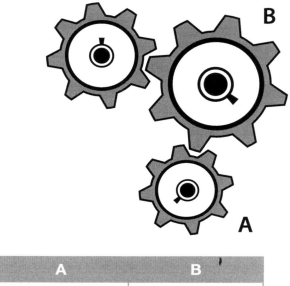

A	B
Clockwise	Anti-clockwise

Question 8

If wheel A is three times the diameter of wheel B and it rotates at 55rpm, what speed will wheel B rotate at?

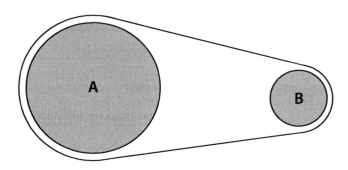

A	B	C
55 rpm	110 rpm	165 rpm

Question 9

How much force is required to lift the 75 kg weight?

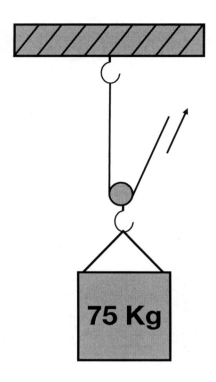

A	B	C	D
15 kg	37.5 kg	75 kg	150 kg

Question 10

A screw has 8 threads per inch. How many full turns are required for the nut to travel 3 inches?

A	B	C	D
8 turns	12 turns	16 turns	24 turns

Question 11

Cog A has 12 teeth and Cog B has 18 teeth. If cog B completes two full turns, how many rotations will Cog A complete?

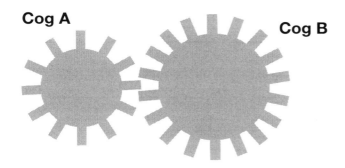

Cog A   **Cog B**

A	B	C	D
3 rotations	2 rotations	1.5 rotations	1 rotation

Question 12

If cog 4 turns anti-clockwise, which other cogs will also turn anti-clockwise?

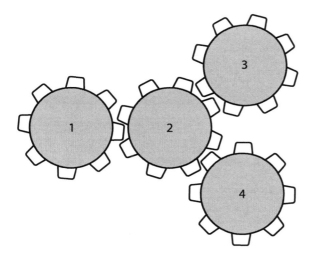

A	B	C	D
Cog 1 only	Cogs 1 and 3	Cog 3 only	Cogs 2 and 3

Question 13

A thick block of wood rests on an even and level sandpaper surface. What mechanical principle makes it difficult to push this block sideways?

A	B	C	D
Spring force	Gravitational force	Air resistance force	Frictional force

Question 14

When water is poured in to a tank, what happens to the pressure on the surface?

A	B	C
Decreases	Stays the same	Increases

Question 15

The following three HGV's are parked on an incline. Their centre of gravity is identified by a dot. Which of the three HGV's is most likely to fall over?

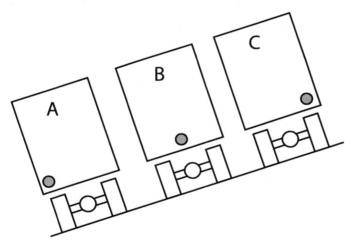

A	B	C
A	B	C

Question 16

Which of the following most resembles a lever?

A = Swing
B = Car
C = Elevator
D = Seesaw

Answer

Question 17

Which tube will the water rise the highest?

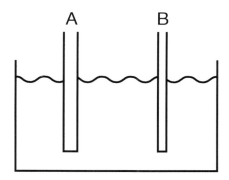

A	B	C	D
Tube A	Tube B	Both the same	Cannot say

Question 18

If the temperature remains constant, what will happen to the volume of trapped gas if the pressure is doubled?

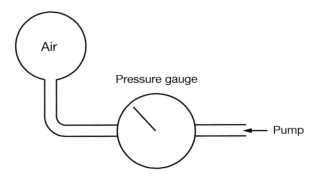

A = the volume it occupies will reduce by 1/3
B = the volume will double
C = the volume will reduce by ¼
D = the volume will reduce by ½

Answer

Question 19

How far would you have to pull the rope up to lift the weight 5 feet?

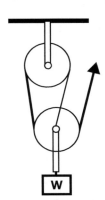

A	B	C	D
5 feet	10 feet	15 feet	30 feet

Question 20

If cog X turns 40 times, how many times will cog Y turn?

A	B	C	D
40 turns	80 turns	120 turns	160 turns

Question 21

Which gate is the strongest?

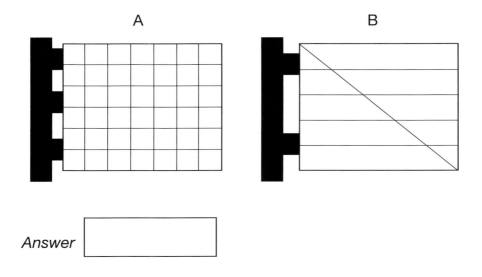

Answer

Question 22

Which of the following pulley systems has a mechanical advantage of 3?

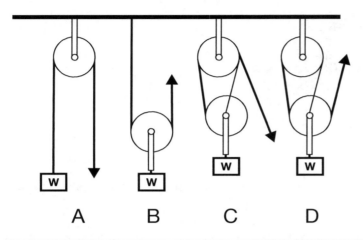

A	B	C	D	E
A and B	C and D	B and D	D	None

Question 23

Which direction should the wind blow in order for the plane to take off with the shortest runway?

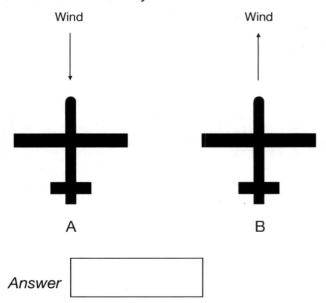

Answer

Question 24

Which wheel will rotate the least number of times in one hour?

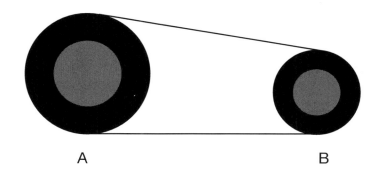

A = Wheel A

B = Wheel B

Answer

Question 25

What shape is the equilibrium?

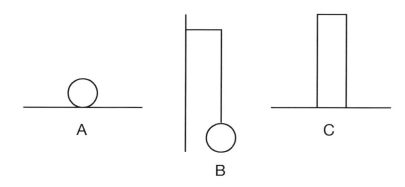

A	B	C	D
Shape A	Shape B	Shape C	All the same

Question 26

If cog C rotates clockwise at a speed of 120 rpm, at what speed and direction will cog A rotate? (rpm = revolutions per minute)

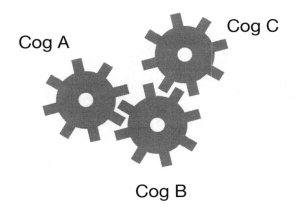

Cog A

Cog C

Cog B

A	B	C	D
120rpm clockwise	120rpm anti-clockwise	40rpm clockwise	40rpm anti-clockwise

Question 27

A cannon is fired from a cannonball horizontally. At the same time you drop a cannon ball of the same weight from the same height. Which will hit the ground first?

A	B	C
Dropped ball	Fired ball	Both the same

Question 28

How much weight in kilograms will need to be added in order to balance the beam?

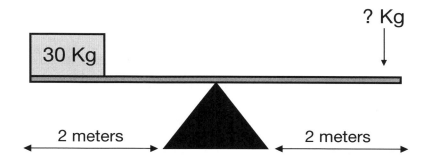

A	B	C	D
10 kg	15 kg	30 kg	60 kg

Question 29

How much weight in kilograms will need to be added in order to balance the beam?

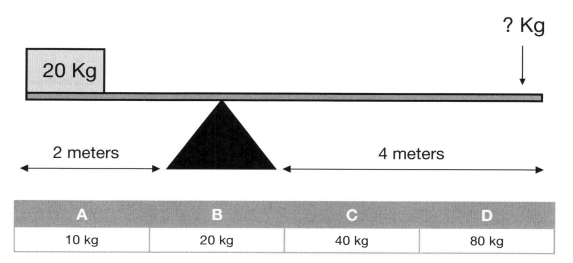

A	B	C	D
10 kg	20 kg	40 kg	80 kg

Question 30

How much weight in kilograms will need to be added in order to balance the beam?

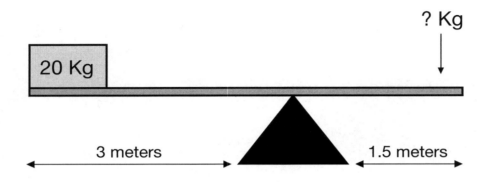

? Kg

20 Kg

3 meters

1.5 meters

A	B	C	D
10 kg	20 kg	30 kg	40 kg

ANSWERS TO MECHANICAL COMPREHENSION – TEST SECTION 1

Q1. A

EXPLANATION = when answering questions where there is a single pulley system, if the pulley is fixed, as in A, then the force required to lift the weight is the same as the weight, i.e. 5kg. However, where the pulley system is not fixed and it moves with the weight, as is the case with pulley system B, then the weight required to lift it is half the weight. This means that the weight required to lift B is 2.5kg. The answer to this question is therefore A, as pulley System A requires the most weight to lift it.

Q2. B = 10 kg

EXPLANATION = Point X is twice the distance from the balance point; therefore, half the weight is required. The answer is B, 10Kg.

Q3. B = 10 rpm/clockwise

EXPLANATION = if cog C turns anti-clockwise at a speed of 10rpm then it is relatively straightforward to determine that cog B will rotate the same speed but in a clockwise direction.

Q4. A = 1

EXPLANATION = the only tool that you can use from the selection to claw nails from wood is claw hammer A.

Q5. D = none

EXPLANATION = no bulbs would illuminate because the circuit, in its current state, is not working. This is due to the switch being open.

Q6. C = two

EXPLANATION = only two bulbs would illuminate (bulbs 1 and 2). The broken circuit would prevent bulb 4 from illuminating.

Q7. A = clockwise

EXPLANATION = Cog A will turn clockwise.

Q8. C = 165 rpm

EXPLANATION = because wheel A is three times greater in diameter than wheel B, each revolution of A will lead to 3 times the revolution of B. Therefore, if wheel A rotates at 55 rpm, B will rotate at 55 rpm × 3 = 165 rpm.

Q9. B = 37.5 kg

EXPLANATION = this type of pulley system has a mechanical advantage of 2. Therefore, to lift the 75 kg weight will require 75 kg ÷ 2 = 37.5 kg.

Q10. D = 24 turns

EXPLANATION = there are 8 threads per inch. To move the nut 3 inches will require 8 × 3 = 24 turns.

Q11. A = 3 rotations

EXPLANATION = each full turn of cog B will result in 18 teeth ÷ 12 teeth = 1.5 rotations. Two turns of cog B will result in cog A completing 3 rotations.

Q12. B = cogs 1 and 3

EXPLANATION = Cogs 1 and 3 will turn anti-clockwise. Cog 2 is the only cog which will rotate clockwise.

Q13. D = frictional force

EXPLANATION = in this particular case frictional force is the force that must be overcome in order to slide the object from one side to another.

Q14. B = stays the same

EXPLANATION = the pressure at the surface remains the same, since there is no water above it.

Q15. A = A

EXPLANATION = by drawing a vertical line straight down from the centre of gravity, only the line for HGV A reaches the ground outside of its tyres. This makes the HGV unstable.

Q16. D = seesaw

EXPLANATION = a seesaw is the only option which utilises a form of leverage to function.

Q17. B = tube B

EXPLANATION = the force between the water and the glass is greater with the narrower tube and so the water will rise higher.

Q18. D = the volume will reduce by ½

EXPLANATION = pressure x volume = constant figure.

Q19. C = 15 feet

EXPLANATION = you would need to lift the rope 15 feet in order to lift the weight 5 feet.

Q20. D = 160 turns

EXPLANATION = Cog X has a total of 20 teeth, whereas cog Y has a total of 5 teeth. Because cog Y has four times fewer teeth than cog X, it will rotate four times for every single full rotation cog X achieves.

Q21. A

EXPLANATION = Gate A is the strongest simply because there are more strengthening points in the construction of the gate and there are also three supporting hinges as opposed to two on gate B.

Q22. D = D

EXPLANATION = only D has a mechanical advantage of 3 as it has three supporting ropes.

Q23. A

EXPLANATION = in order to take-off with the shortest runway the aircraft will require a head wind.

Q24. A = wheel A

EXPLANATION = Wheel A is the largest and will therefore rotate the least number of times in any given time-frame.

Q25. D = all the same

EXPLANATION = all three are in the equilibrium state because none of them are moving.

Q26. A = 120 rpm/clockwise

EXPLANATION = Cog A will rotate 120 rpm clockwise. It is advisable to count the number of teeth on each. In this particular scenario, each cog has the same number of teeth; therefore, the cogs will rotate at the same speed.

Q27. C = both the same

EXPLANATION = they will both hit the ground at the same time.

Q28. C = 30 kg

EXPLANATION = the distance of the weights from the fulcrum/balance point is identical; therefore, the weight required to balance the beam should be identical.

Q29. A = 10 kg

EXPLANATION = the distance of the weights from the fulcrum/balance point is double; therefore, the weight required to balance the beam should be halved.

Q30. D = 40 kg

EXPLANATION = the distance of the weights from the fulcrum/balance point is halved; therefore, the weight required to balance the beam should be doubled.

MECHANICAL COMPREHENSION - TEST 2

(You have 10 minutes in which to complete the 30 questions).

Question 1

In electrical circuits, the diagram below is used to represent what?

A	B	C	D
Bulb	Battery	Resister	Switch

Question 2

If input effort is 600 ft.lb, what output effort will be produced by a machine with a mechanical advantage of 4?

Answer

Question 3

Which of the pendulums will swing at the fastest speed?

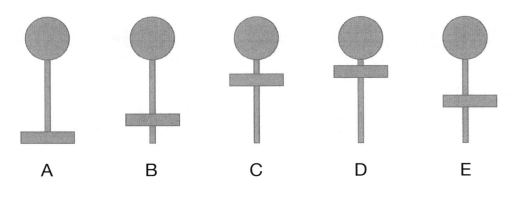

A   B   C   D   E

Answer

Question 4

At which point(s) should air enter the cylinder in order to force the piston downwards?

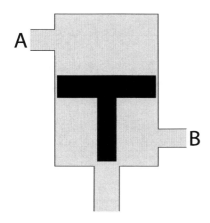

A	B	C
Point A	Point B	Points A and B

Question 5

At what point would the beam balance?

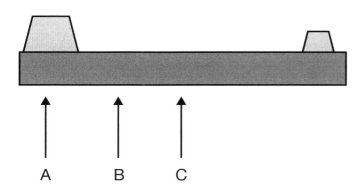

A	B	C
Point A	Point B	Point C

Question 6

How much weight is required to balance the load?

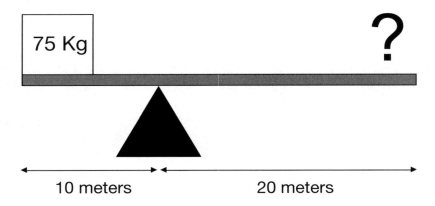

A	B	C	D
37.5 kg	75 kg	125.5 kg	150 kg

Question 7

If gear A in the diagram begins spinning clockwise, what will happen to the spring that is attached to the wall?

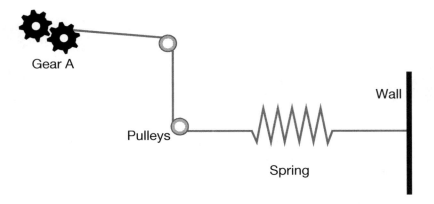

A	B	C	D
The spring will be compressed	The spring will stretch	The spring will touch the gears	Nothing

Question 8

Which tank will not empty?

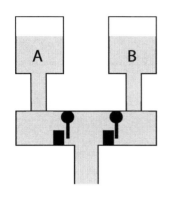

A	B	C
Tank A	Tank B	Both the same

Question 9

Which crane is working under the least tension?

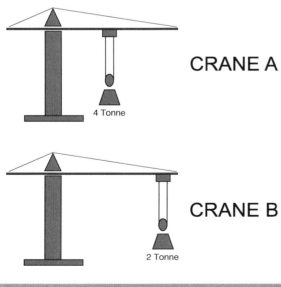

A	B	C
Crane A	Crane B	Both the same

Question 10

Which of the following statements will increase the mechanical advantage of this inclined plane?

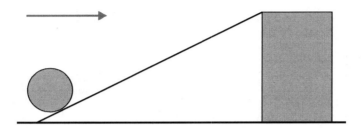

A – Shorten the length of the ramp

B – Make the ramp longer

C – Increase the slope of the ramp

D - Lessen the force acting at the arrow

Answer [   ]

Question 11

If the object on the left side of the scale is 72 ft. away from the balance point, i.e. the fulcrum, and a force is applied 8 ft. from the fulcrum on the right side, what is the mechanical advantage?

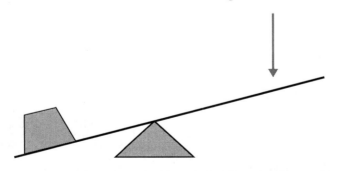

A	B	C	D
9	4.5	18	36

Question 12

Which type of beam can take the greatest load?

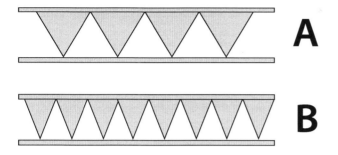

A = Beam A

B = Beam B

C = Both the same

Answer

Question 13

Which cog will make the most number of turns in 30 seconds?

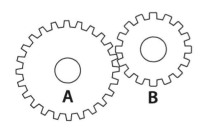

A	B	C
Cog A	Cog B	Both the same

Question 14

At what point would you need to place weight X in order for the scales to balance?

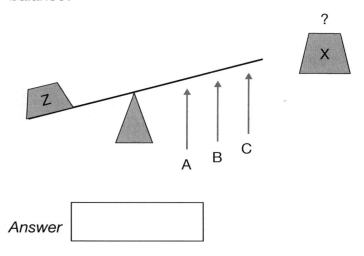

Answer [   ]

Question 15

A force of 15 kg compresses the springs. What will be the total distance that the springs in parallel are compressed?

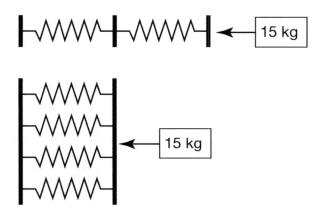

A	B	C	D
2.5 cm	10 cm	7.5 cm	4.5 cm

Question 16

How much force is required to move the following weight?

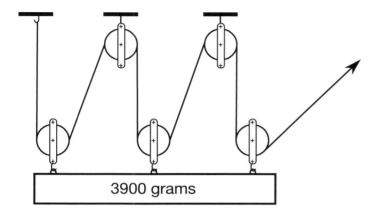

A	B	C	D
65 grams	1950 grams	650 grams	4000 grams

Question 17

Which weight requires the least amount of force?

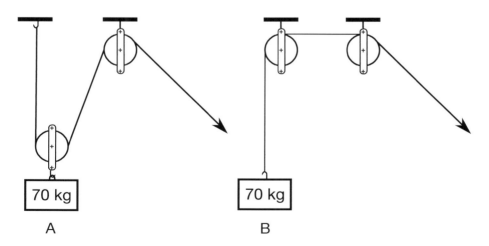

A	B
70 kg	70 kg
A	B

A	B	C
Both the same	A	B

Question 18

How many switches need to be closed to light up one bulb?

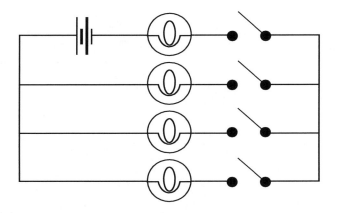

A	B	C	D
1	2	3	4

Question 19

In the diagram, the spring can be stretched 1 inch by a force of 200 pounds. How much force needs to be applied to the object in order to move the object 4.5 inches to the left?

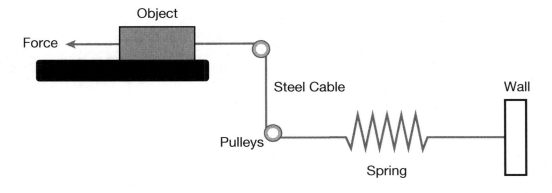

A	B	C	D
900 pounds	450 pounds	800 pounds	90 pounds

Question 20

What would happen to a balloon full of air, if you were to place it 15 feet below a water surface?

A – The volume of the balloon would increase
B – The volume of the balloon would stay the same
C – The balloon would explode
D – The volume of the balloon would decrease

Answer

Question 21

If bar X moves right at a constant speed, how does bar Y move?

A	B	C	D
Right, faster	Right, slower	Right, same	Left, same

Question 22

Which is the most suitable tool for breaking up concrete?

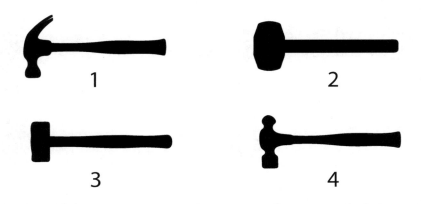

A	B	C	D
1	2	3	4

Question 23

Which hammer is most suitable for general work with metal?

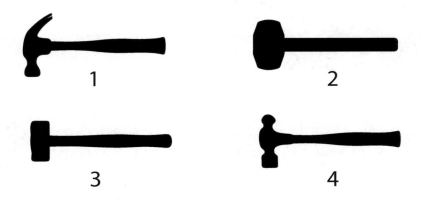

A	B	C	D
1	2	3	4

Question 24

If water was poured in at point Z, which point would take longest to fill up?

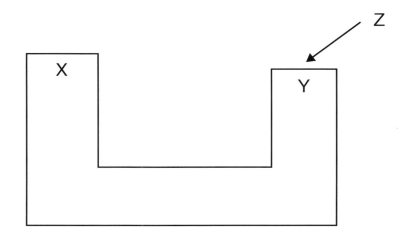

A	B	C
Tube X	Tube Y	Both the same

Question 25

Which of the shelves can carry the heaviest load?

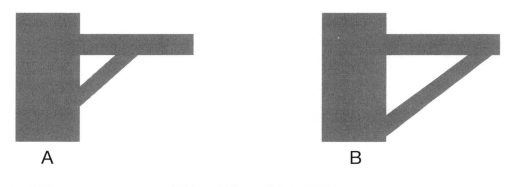

A	B	C
Shelf A	Shelf B	Both the same

Question 26

Which rope (A, B or C) would be the easiest to pull the mass object over?

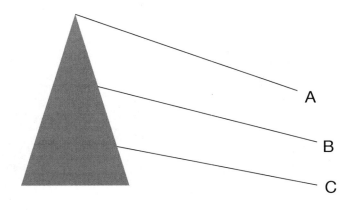

A	B	C	D
Rope A	Rope B	Rope C	Rope B and C

Question 27

At which point will a ball travel at the slowest speed?

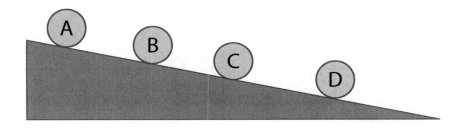

A	B	C	D	E
Ball A	Ball B	Ball C	Ball D	All the same

Question 28

If circle Y rotates anti-clockwise, what way will circle X rotate?

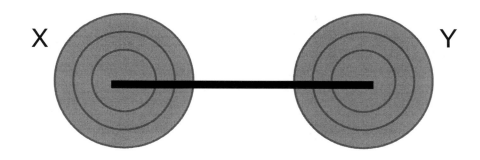

A	B	C
Clockwise	Anti-clockwise	Cannot say

Question 29

In the diagram, two wheels attached by a belt drive have the ratio of 3 : 1. The smaller wheel has a 10cm circumference. How fast would the smaller wheel turn if the larger wheel turned at a rate of 450 rpm.

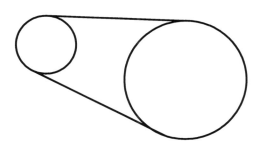

A	B	C	D
1300 rpm	1350 rpm	750 rpm	700 rpm

Question 30

How much force is required to lift the weights?

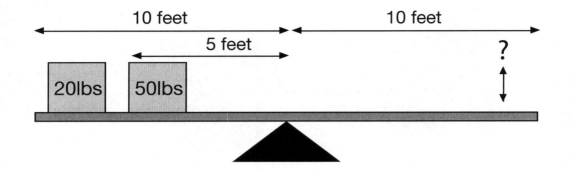

A	B	C	D
20 lbs	70 lbs	35 lbs	45 lbs

ANSWERS TO MECHANICAL COMPREHENSION – TEST SECTION 2

Q1. B = battery
EXPLANATION = the diagram is used to represent a battery.

Q2. A = 2400 ft. lb.
EXPLANATION = 600 x 4 = 2400 ft. lb.

Q3. D
EXPLANATION = the fastest swinging pendulum will be figure D. The position of the rectangle determines how fast the pendulum will swing. Figure A would swing the slowest, because the rectangle is at its lowest point in Figure A. The higher the rectangle, the faster the pendulum will swing.

Q4. A = point A
EXPLANATION = for air to be forced downwards, the air needs to enter the cylinder from Point A. If it was to enter from Point B, the air would be forced upwards.

Q5. B = Point B
EXPLANATION = the beam would balance at Point B.

Q6. A = 37.5 kg
EXPLANATION = the distance of the weights from the fulcrum/balance point is double; therefore, the weight required to balance the beam should be halved.

Q7. B = the spring will stretch
EXPLANATION = if the gears moved in a clockwise manner, that means that the cable connecting everything together is going to move left (towards the gears), and so the spring will stretch as the cable is being tightened.

Q8. B = Tank B
EXPLANATION = Tank B will not empty because the valve will not permit water to flow past it.

Q9. C = both the same

EXPLANATION = they are both under the same tension. Although the weight lifted by crane A is double that of crane B, the weight is closer to the centre of gravity.

Q10. B = make the ramp longer

EXPLANATION = the mechanical advantage of an inclined plane can be worked out by dividing the effort of the distance by the resistant distance. In other words, the ratio of this formula must increase which means making the distance longer i.e. lengthening the ramp.

Q11. A = 9

EXPLANATION = the effort force where the weight is to be applied (where the arrow is pointing) is equal to the resistance weight of the object on the left side of the scales. To work out the mechanical advantage, you can use the following formula: divide the length of the effort by the length of the resistance. So, $72 \div 8 = 9$. Thus, the mechanical advantage is 9.

Q12 A = Beam A

EXPLANATION = Beam A is the strongest because each triangular section covers a greater surface area.

Q13. B = Cog B

EXPLANATION = the cog with the fewest teeth will make the most number of turns in any given time-frame. Because cog B has fewer teeth, it will complete more turns than cog A.

Q14. A

EXPLANATION = in order for the scales to balance, the weight would need to be positioned at point A.

Q15. C = 7.5 cm

EXPLANATION = in order for the springs to be compressed in parallel with one another, the springs will need to be compressed by half, so they will be compressed by 7.5 cm.

Q16. C = 650 grams

EXPLANATION = the weight of the object is 3900 grams. There are 6 sections (parts of the rope) supporting the weight. So, you need to divide 3900 by 6 to generate your answer. 3900 ÷ 6 = 650 grams.

Q17. B = A

EXPLANATION = Weight A requires a force equal to 37.5kg, whereas weight B requires a force equal to 70kg.

Q18. B = 2

EXPLANATION = two switches need to be closed in order to light up one bulb. Two switches and one bulb makes up one complete circuit.

Q19. A = 900 pounds

EXPLANATION = 4.5 multiplied by 200 = 900 pounds.

Q20. D = the volume of the balloon would decrease

EXPLANATION = if you were to place a balloon full of air 15 feet under a water surface, the volume of the balloon would decrease. The pressure on the balloon from the water would press inwards, and therefore it would cause the balloon to shrink in size and subsequently decrease the volume of the balloon.

Q21. C = right, same

EXPLANATION = if bar X moves at a constant speed, using the cogs in between, you can see that they will move at the same speed (count the number of teeth on each; the two large cogs are the same size, and the two smaller ones are also the same size). Therefore, bar Y has to move in the same direction at the same speed.

Q22. B = 2

EXPLANATION = the most suitable tool to break up concrete would be item number 2 (a sledge hammer).

Q23. D = 4

EXPLANATION = the most suitable hammer to do general work with metal is item number 4 (a ball-peen hammer).

Q24. A = tube X

EXPLANATION = If water was being poured in from Point Z, Tube X would take the longest to fill up because it is the tube that is the biggest.

Q25. B = shelf B

EXPLANATION = the shelf that can carry the most weight is shelf B. The bar underneath, holding the shelf up is positioned better in order to hold more weight. Shelf A has the diagonal bar positioned in the middle, and therefore a lot of weight on the shelf would cause the shelf to collapse on the right side.

Q26. Rope A

EXPLANATION = rope A is positioned best to pull over the mass object. The rope is positioned at the mass' weakest point (the smallest point), and so it would be the easiest place to pull over the object.

Q27. A = Ball A

EXPLANATION = you need to work out which position the ball will be moving at the slowest speed. Note, this question is not asking you about four separate balls, it is asking you about one ball and each stage of the ball being rolled down the slope. So, the slowest point at which the ball will be rolling is point A; point D will be the fastest.

Q28. B = anti-clockwise

EXPLANATION = the straight line running through the centre of both circles indicates that both circles will rotate the same way. Therefore, both circles will be rotating anti-clockwise.

Q29. B = 1350 rpm

EXPLANATION = the large wheel rotates three times less than the smaller wheel. So, if the larger wheel is rotating at 450 rpm, this means that the smaller wheel must be rotating at a rate three times faster. So, 450 x 3 = 1350 rpm.

Q30. D = 45 lbs

EXPLANATION = $f = (20 \times 10) + (50 \times 5) \div 10$
$f = (200) + (250) \div 10$
$f = 450 \div 10$ 45 lbs.

A FEW
FINAL WORDS...

You have now reached the end of your Royal Navy Recruiting test. Now, you should feel more confident and capable of tackling your Royal Navy Recruiting test. We hope you have found this guide an invaluable insight into the type of test you will face during the application process of joining the Royal Navy.

For any psychometric test, there are a few things to remember to help you perform at your best...

REMEMBER – THE THREE P'S!

1. **Prepare.** This may seem relatively obvious, but you will be surprised by how many people fail psychometric testing because they lacked knowledge and understanding of what to expect. Be sure to practice these tests before having to sit your real test. Not only will you become familiar with the testing questions, it will also take off some of the pressure leading up to that all important test. Like anything, the more you practice, the more likely you are to succeed!

2. **Perseverance.** Everybody comes across setbacks in their life, or times when there are obstacles in the way of their goals. The important thing to remember when this happens, is to use those setbacks and obstacles as a way of progressing. It is what you do with your past experiences that helps to determine your success in the future. If you fail at something, consider 'why' you have failed. This will allow you to improve and enhance your performance for next time.

3. **Performance.** Your performance will determine whether or not you are likely to succeed. Attributes that are often associated with performance are self-belief, motivation and commitment. Self-belief is important for anything you do in your life. It allows you to recognise your own abilities and skills and believe that you can do well. Believing that you can do well is half the battle! Being fully motivated and committed is often difficult for some people, but we can assure you that, nothing is gained without hard work and determination. If you want to succeed, you will need to put in that extra time and hard work!

Work hard, stay focused, and be what you want!

Good luck with your Royal Navy Recruiting test. We wish you the best of luck with all your future endeavours!

The how2become team

The How2become team

how2become

Get more books, manuals, online tests and training courses at:

www.How2Become.com